JESUS CHRIST

OR

MOHAMMED?

F.S Coplestone B.D. grew up in Wrexham, Wales. At the age of nineteen, he became a local preacher. His full-time ministry began in 1928, after three years training at the Porth Bible Training Institute and continued until 1972. As well as being a pastor he was a tutor in New Testament Greek in the Porth Bible Training Institute and, later, in Apologetics and Non-Christian Religions at the Barry Bible College. He died in the summer of 1998 at the age of 95.

JESUS CHRIST

OR

MOHAMMED?

The Bible
or
the Koran?

F.S. Coplestone

CHRISTIAN FOCUS

10 9 8 7 6 5 4 3 2 1

ISBN 1 85792 588 2

First published in 2000
and reprinted in 2001, 2002 and 2006
by
Christian Focus Publications
Geanies House, Fearn, Ross-shire,
IV20 1TW, Great Britain.

www.christianfocus.com

Cover design by Danie Van Straaten

Printed and bound by
Nørhaven Paperback A/S, Denmark

This small book has been edited and expanded with the desire to
reach others with the love of Christ.

Contents

1

Understanding the Test of True Religion

There are many religions that claim to be the one and only true religion. Since this is the case, there needs to be a test of Divine truth to which the claims of all religions can be submitted. Logic states that it can only be God who supplies this test. God is our creator, and has made us with the ability to acquire knowledge and communicate with one another. Since God is so far above us (being the one who made the universe), knowledge of Him can only come through His own revelation of Himself. It is from this revelation that we must find the test of all true religion.

The Test of True Religion
The most important test of true religion is the Law of God that says: 'Love the LORD your God with all your heart and with all your soul and with all your strength,' and 'Love your neighbour as yourself' (Deut. 6:5; 10:12, 19; 11:1; 13:3; 30:16; Lev. 19:18; Matt. 22:37, 39).

God has said that perfect obedience to this Law of Love is the necessary condition to receiving eternal life: 'Keep my decrees and laws, for the man who obeys them will live by them. I am the LORD' (Lev. 18:5).

We also find that God has pronounced His curse on all who break this Law. This is necessary and shows how right and perfect He is. It reveals God's hostility to the rebellion of disobedience. Rebellion reveals that we believe that we can live our lives as we please. However, the evil in our world reveals that we fail to even live by our own standards, let alone God's. Due to sin, we are under the condemnation of the Holy One whose ways are far above our own. 'Cursed is the man who does not uphold the words of this law by carrying them out' (Deut. 27:26).

As sinners, it is impossible for us to obtain (or even help to obtain) eternal life by our own good works. We are imperfect and can never pay a perfect price, no matter how hard we work. Our best is still not good enough, and is tainted by sin. We cannot escape from being under the condemnation of a Holy God. Therefore, if we are to meet the demands of his law, we need to be totally dependent on Him. We are not capable of living by His rule of love, on which our thinking and behaviour is to be based. Neither can we pay the penalty for our wrongdoing. Yet there is hope.

The Law of Love Reveals that God is Love

Human laws are undeniable evidence of both the existence and character of human lawgivers. The types of laws they give tell us something about the lawgiver. For example, someone who makes harsh and legalistic rulings is often harsh and legalistic by nature. From this we can see that, in a much greater way, God's Law of Love is the undeniable evidence of both the existence and character of God. Only a God who is Love by nature could require everyone to love Him and their fellow man.

The nature of love is to give out of oneself for others – to meet the needs of a loved one with the best of our ability, regardless of cost. This Law of Love assures us that God wants to meet the need of every sinner, because He loves us (whilst hating our sin). It is impossible for a holy and perfect God to command everyone to love Him, unless He Himself loves everyone. If God did not love everyone He would be a hypocrite, since God would have asked us to do something He had no intention of doing Himself. God is perfect and holy, and His Law of Love reveals that He is not like this.

Since God is Love (1 John 4:8), and loves everyone, He must have provided salvation for every sinner who takes up his offer of life. Love does not forsake a loved one. And so we see that God's Law of Love is a prophecy of the good news (gospel) of God's redemption (buying back those in slavery) for the human race.

The one and only true religion will be the one that reveals and proclaims that God has provided full redemption (paid the full price) for sinners. This comes about by His grace (undeserved favour) alone.

If God had deliberately made some people with no ability to love Him, then their not loving Him could not be called sin. Scripture informs us that 'all have sinned and fall short of the glory of God' (Rom. 3:23), and that 'Everyone who sins breaks the law' (1 John 3:4). Therefore it is everyone's responsibility to keep the Law of Love.

Scriptures and experience show that all enjoy the blessings of providence as gifts of grace, not through their own merit:

'The LORD is good to all; he has compassion on all he has made' (Ps. 145:9).

To say that the Lord is good and merciful to all, but does not love all is to say that goodness and mercy are not attributes of His love. Attributes are qualities of nature or substance, and do not stand separately on their own.

Continuing to look at love, one realises that love's greatest revelation lies in its greatest possible sacrifice, for all sacrifice is personal. What was necessary for our salvation was God's judgement on sin and the execution of the curse of the Law to come about in a way that would not condemn us. This was achieved by Jesus' perfect obedience to God's will. Jesus became the sin-bearer for us. God could make no greater revelation of His love to sinners than the sacrifice of His eternal Son.

The Law of Love Refutes the Unitarian Doctrine of God

The doctrine of God in both Judaism and the Koran is Unitarian. However, the Law of Love proves that there is a plurality of Persons within the Unity of the Godhead. This must be so because love must have an object, since it is a relationship between a lover and a loved one. Therefore, eternal love is an eternal relationship in God. For this reason some Moslems deny that Allah loves.

The eternal object of God's love cannot be outside the Godhead, because this would mean that God is wholly dependent upon some other eternal Being for the object and reciprocation of His love. God, then being dependent on something outside of Himself, would no longer be self-sufficient or independent. Also, if there were two beings, then neither would be almighty. Neither would have any control over the other and there would be no 'moral absolute'. From this we see how the Unitarian doctrine of God makes God dependent upon His creation for the object and reciprocation of His love, and denies that God is love *by nature*. It would mean that God's love is not eternal, it no longer being something that speaks to us of the very essence of God. Instead, it would be potential, and not necessary to God's Being.

Our idea of love is formed from the relationships around us, and our ability to love is often dependent on others returning our love. This is not the case with God. He is an infinitely perfect Being who is love by nature, this being the very essence of His Being. This is why scripture tells us that 'God is Love' (1 John 4:8) and does not say 'Love is God.' God does not love us because of what we can do for Him in the way of good works. Neither did God create us to make up for any lack within Himself. God is eternal love within His own Being. He created a world and placed man within creation so that mankind could benefit from His love. He does not need us; is not dependent on our world in any way, and loves us because He simply chooses to love. We have been created by God to benefit from His love.

Most human beings can love a small baby, which can do little more than lie in our arms. God's love is far greater than this, for no effect (my loving a child) is greater that the cause (He giving me the ability to love in the first place).

From all that we have said so far, we see that the concept of God as an independent self-sufficient Being is far greater than that of a God who is dependent upon His own creation for the object and reciprocation of His love.

Dr Hutton in *Theological Essays* says that his

conversion from Unitarianism to belief in God as triune, (as revealed in the Bible), came about when he saw that, in God, love must be eternal. Since love is eternal it obviously speaks of the existence of eternal relationships within the Godhead.

The Law of Love Provides Evidence of Supernatural Revelation

The Law of Love is completely beyond the power and ability of any sinner to keep. It is so contrary to human nature, that we can be certain that it did not originate with man, because obedience to it requires sinless perfection. Apart from this, it is not possible for someone to have forged a Law of Love. Forgers (creators of false information) forge documents that are for self-gain, they are not in the least concerned with love, either to God or to their fellow man.

The Law of Love speaks of the inner motives of heart and mind, and goes far beyond outward actions, which can be deceptive. God requires love to Him as the supreme motive behind all our actions and as the inspiration of all our thoughts and words. Whatever is not motivated by love to Him is sin – it breaks the first and greatest commandment of His Law. Understanding this, and knowing God's demands, effectively removes all claims to self-righteousness, and reliance on any form of good works for salvation. After all, Jesus taught that God's Law can be broken inwardly, even when there is the outward appearance of keeping it. What might appear and feel good to us can be an abomination in the sight of God.

> 'You are the ones who justify yourselves in the eyes of men, but God knows your hearts. What is highly valued among men is detestable in God's sight' (Luke 16:15).

Perfect obedience to God's Law of Love is the only means of justification before God.

It is the only condition whereby we can receive eternal life. If God did not judge sin, then He would sacrifice any claim to being righteous, yet it was impossible for any man to keep His law since no sinner can offer sinless perfection. If there were to be a Saviour for mankind the Saviour would have to be a sinless representative. His righteousness would then be that of perfect obedience to the Law of Love and could be credited to mankind. However, since the wrath of God is infinite (boundless/ incalculable), this Saviour would also need to be Deity incarnate. After all, only a Divine being could offer anything acceptable enough to deliver sinners from judgement and, in doing so, obtain forgiveness of sins for them. The union of Deity with His humanity made it possible for all that Jesus achieved (paying for our sins) to be passed on to all who accept His saving work.

I once read a story where a judge had to pass sentence on a friend who had committed a crime. Those who heard about the forthcoming case were divided into two camps. On the one side there were those who thought the judge would be a good judge and stick to the rules in passing sentence. But they were aware that this would mean that he was not a very good friend. Others thought that the judge would let his friend off without having to pay a penalty. Yet they realised that, in being a good friend, he was not a good judge. When the case came to court, both groups found that they were wrong.

After hearing the case, the judge stood up and fined his friend the maximum penalty for committing the crime. He then took of his robes, walked down to his friend and took out his chequebook in order to pay the fine himself. He was both a good judge and a good friend.

In Jesus Christ we have a Saviour who shows us that God is both righteous and merciful.

Representation and Imputation
(To 'impute' means to 'reckon to one' and, in scripture, refers to the righteousness of Christ being imputed (reckoned) to us.)

The fact that God is Love (as the Law of Love reveals) proves that suffering and death have no place in His universe, apart from sin. Yet infants, who have no personal sin, are still subject to suffering and death even before birth. How is this so?

Adam and Eve were the first of our species of being, therefore, when sin entered their lives it would affect all offspring as well. Every human being is born 'diseased', and with the potential for sin within him, including babies. Although they have broken no moral law, the disease of sin has been passed to them. Their bodies are no longer capable of living forever and death can ensue at any time. When full judgement comes from God it will not arise because of Adam's sins, but because of our own sins, committed because we are part of Adam's 'fallen' race. All have sinned and fall short of the glory of God (Rom. 3:23).

Sinners cannot obtain perfect human righteousness. Therefore it was necessary for a sinless representative to come as a man, live a life of perfect obedience to the Law, and then have His righteousness imputed to all related to Him. This relationship is established through faith alone, with no personal merit involved.

Substitutionary and Non-Substitutionary Representation
(When one man pays another man's fine in a law court, he is said to have represented him substitutionally.)
It was necessary that the Divine side of the Redeemer's work should be substitutionary in order to save us from bearing the wrath of God by ourselves. Yet it was also necessary that the human side of the Redeemer's work (obtaining eternal life by obedience to the law of love) should be non-substitutionary. The purpose of Christ's obedience was to obtain eternal life as a free gift

of God's grace. We could then live a life of love by His power.

Those who are redeemed are then called to love as they have been loved. Their good works do not maintain salvation – since every sin has been paid for – yet the works reveal the wonderful love that has been received through salvation.

The Necessity of Restitution to Redemption
(Restitution speaks of the act of restoring to the rightful owner something that has been lost or stolen, whilst Redemption means 'to deliver from', and refers, in the Bible, to the believer having been delivered from sin.)

Man's disobedience has robbed God of honour and glory which obedience would have brought to Him. Therefore the Divine plan of redemption (delivering man from sin) needs to restore to God all the honour and glory lost through man breaking the Law of Love. If this were not so then God would be the eternal loser (as a result of man's sin), which is impossible. In light of this, the one true religion, (based only on supernatural revelation), needs to reveal that the Divine plan of salvation has restored to God all honour and glory lost through man's sin. Any doctrine of salvation that fails to do this cannot be true.

In order to be able to love, one has to have freedom of choice since you cannot force a person to love you. God created us to benefit from His love, and in giving us freedom of choice allows the possibility of evil. God's permission of evil has caused great loss to Him, and great misery and sorrow and spiritual loss for the human race. It can only be justified if God overrules it to secure greater glory to His Name. It secures, but only for those who believe in Him, greater blessing for those who previously suffered misery, sorrow and spiritual loss. Therefore the one true religion must also reveal the way in which God has overruled evil, securing greater honour and glory to His name than if He had never permitted it to exist in His Universe at all.

The First Announcements Concerning the Law of Love

The Law of Love was given to our first parents at their creation to reveal to them the nature of God and His will for their lives (1 John 3:11, 12). God's command, which warned them not to take anything from the tree of the knowledge of good and evil (Gen. 2:16, 17), was given to test their love for God. This was because there is no virtue in untested obedience. Only by overcoming the temptation to disobedience could innocence (a negative quality) develop into righteousness (a positive quality) which is an active, thinking and deliberate conforming to God's standard.

Our first parents were created in the image of God as moral beings, in contrast to the animal creation (Gen. 1:26). They also had the capacity to become the image of God as righteous beings by victory over temptation. Disobedience made them sinful by nature, whilst obedience would have made them righteous by nature, and secured them eternal life, which would also have been transmitted to their descendants.

Paul tells us that the Law was given for life (Rom. 7:10). Due to the corruption of human nature it became impossible for men and women to gain eternal life by their own obedience to God's law. Instead, they were now brought under condemnation from which only God could deliver them.

The purpose in giving the Law to the nation of Israel through Moses at Sinai (Exod. 20:1-17) was to teach them that they could not bring about their own deliverance. This would help prepare them to receive God's plan of salvation by grace (undeserved favour) through faith in the Redeemer whom God would send. As we have already stated, God's own Law of Love assured them that He would provide for sinners.

The Redemption of Creation
Redemption would be incomplete unless it included the whole terrestrial creation involved in the consequences of man's sin. The creation (being subject to the curse, due to man's sin) is, through God's saving work, that of 'groaning as in the pains of childbirth right up to the present time' (Rom. 8:22).

The Need for Preparatory Revelation

The Law of Love, (revealing God as love), assures us that God would provide information of His intention to redeem man, right at the beginning of man's experience as a sinner. Man would know about the promised Redeemer and the way in which the Redeemer would accomplish His work of Redemption. This is so that mankind could exercise faith in Him and receive the benefits of that Redemption even before it occurred.

Therefore, another hallmark of the one true religion will be that God's purpose to redeem mankind would be known from the beginning. Along with this would be known something of the Person of the Redeemer and the way in which He would accomplish Redemption.

2

The Doctrine of God

In the Koran, God (Allah) is declared to be
Omnipotent (All-powerful), Omniscient, (All
knowing), and Omnipresent which means
'everywhere present' (Suras 57:4; 6:59; 58:6).

He is also said to be the Creator (Sura 6:101),
perfect in all His works (67:3); He provides for
all (15:20; 17:21, 31) and is the one who does
not change (48:23). He is the First and the Last
(57:3); Forgiving (5:98); Mighty and Wise (60:5);
the Compassionate and the Merciful (at the head
of every Sura). All Christians agree that God is like
this. However the Koran also says that God is said
to mislead (35:8; 13:27), and to have predestined
every act, both good and bad (91:8; 14:4, 32),
which, as we shall see, is against the teaching of
the Scriptures.

Many Suras speak of God's love, but none
speak of God loving the undeserving, and the
unrighteous, as a merciful God would do.

The Doctrine of Divine Unity

The Koranic doctrine of God is Unitarian. His Unity is a mathematical Unity, as opposed to the unity of created life, even the life of a plant, which is complex. The Deity of Christ is expressly denied, and the Holy Spirit is identified with the angel Gabriel.

Sura 2:116:   They say: 'God hath begotten a son': Glory be to Him, Nay, to Him belongs all that is in the heavens and on earth: everything renders worship to Him.

6:101:   To Him is due the primal origin of the heavens and the earth: How can He have a son when He hath no consort? He created all things, and He hath full knowledge of all things. (This shows Mohammed took his idea of sonship from human relationships. Like the Jews he could not conceive of spiritual relationships within the Godhead.)

19:35:   It is not befitting to (the majesty of) God that He should beget a son. Glory be to Him! When He determines a matter, He only says to it, 'Be', and it is.

19:88:   They say, '(God) Most Gracious Has begotten a son!'

37:151,152:   Is it not that they say, from their

own invention, 'God has begotten children'? But they are liars!

39:4: Had God wished to take to Himself a son, He could have chosen whom he pleased out of those whom He doth create: but Glory be to Him! (He is above such things.) He is God, the One, the Irresistible.

16:51: God has said: 'Take not (for worship) two gods: For He is just One God: Then fear Me (and Me alone).'

Sura 9:30: The Jews call Uzair a son of God, and the Christians call Christ the Son of God. That is a saying from their mouth; (in this) they but imitate what the Unbelievers of old used to say. God's curse be on them: how they are deluded away from the Truth!

23:91: No son did God beget, nor is there any god along with Him: (if there were many gods), behold each god would have taken away what he had created, and some would have lorded it over others! Glory to God! (He is free) from the (sort of) things they attribute to Him!

5:119: And behold! God will say: 'O Jesus the son of Mary! Didst thou say unto men, worship me and my mother as gods in derogation of God'?'

He will say: 'Glory to Thee! Never could I say what I had no right (to say). Had I said such a thing, Thou wouldst indeed have known it. Thou knowest what is in my heart, though I know not what is in Thine. For Thou knowest in full all that is hidden.'

In Mohammed's day there were those who wrongly stated that the Trinity consisted of the Father, Son and Virgin Mary. No Christian has ever believed this. Yet Mohammed believed this to be true. He had no firsthand knowledge of the Scriptures, never speaking to true Christians. In the Koran he condemned this view of the Trinity, which no Christian has ever held to. Concerning this view Zechariah Butrus writes in his book (*God is One in the Holy Trinity*, p. 30):

Before Islam in the fifth century AD, a heretical doctrine appeared. The adherents of this doctrine were heathens who embraced Christianity. As pagans they worshipped the planet Venus and said that it was 'the Queen of Heaven.' After embracing Christianity they tried to associate what they had worshipped with Christian doctrine. They considered Mary as 'Queen of Heaven' or 'Goddess of Heaven' instead of Venus. Consequently, the called themselves Mariamists. They came to believe that there are three gods: God, Mary, and Christ.

Christians have always seen this doctrine as utterly false, and unscriptural. Christians believe as strongly as Mohammed did that there is only one God.

In Mohammed's day many false doctrines were being spoken about as if they were Christian truth. History reveals that several Church councils had already been called to deal with errors concerning the Trinity, and the person of Christ – relating to both His Deity and His humanity.

God as Loving, Merciful and Gracious

Muslim theologians do not accept the Plurality of Persons in the Unity of the Godhead, yet recognise that love desires the reciprocation of love. Therefore, to preserve God's independence and self-sufficiency they deny that God loves. To quote Dr Elder from *Biblical Approach to the Moslem*, the Moslems argue that 'to love is to sense the need of the beloved. And since God cannot be said to have a need, it is impossible for God to love.' Yet this view denies many statements in the Koran which assert that God does indeed love. Therefore this view forfeits, for them, any true claim to be Moslem. This forfeit is because belief in the Koran, as an absolute perfect revelation, is the foundation of the Moslem religion.

3:31:   Say: 'If ye do love God, follow me: God will love you and forgive you your sins: For God is Oft-Forgiving, Most Merciful.'

3:57:   As to those who believe and work righteousness, God will pay them (in full) their reward; but God loveth not those who do wrong.

3:134:   Those who spend (freely), whether in prosperity, or in adversity; who restrain anger, and pardon (all) men; for God loves those who do good;

3:146:   How many of the Prophets fought (in God's way), and with them (fought) large bands of godly men? But they never lost heart if they met with disaster in God's way, nor did they weaken (in will) nor give in. And God loves those who are firm and steadfast.

3: 148.   And God gave them a reward in this world, and the excellent reward of the Hereafter. For God loveth those who do good.

2: 218:   Those who believed and those who suffered exile and fought (and strove and struggled) in the path of God, – they have the hope of the Mercy of God: And God is Oft-forgiving, Most Merciful.

In addition to these Suras (which refer to God as loving) there are many references in the Koran to God's mercifulness and graciousness, which are attributes of love. Yet, in the Koran, this mercy is limited to the deserving, which perverts the meaning of mercy. The very nature of mercy speaks of loving the undeserving, and grace and mercy exclude merit. Meanwhile, we find that the Bible recognises the love of God to those who deserve nothing, who through trusting in Christ's saving work, can receive everything:

> But God demonstrates his own love for us in this: While we were still sinners, Christ died for us (Rom. 5:8).

> For if, when we were God's enemies, we were reconciled to him through the death of his Son, how much more, having been reconciled, shall we be saved through his life! (Rom. 5:10).

According to the Koran, the love of God is conditional upon merit in the individual believing in God along with accompanying good works. Yet the Law of Love given to sinners actually proves that His love, as grace and mercy, extends to everyone. Those who love God still need the love of His grace in salvation so that they can actually meet with God. This does not come about through good works, which could never appease the wrath of a Holy God. The claims of the Koran to be Divine revelation are disproved by making grace and mercy in God dependent on merit.

The following Suras refer to Allah's grace and mercy:

2:105:   It is never the wish of those without faith among the People of the Book, nor of the Pagans, that anything good should come down to you from your Lord. But God will choose for His Special Mercy whom he will – for God is Lord of grace abounding.

4:95:   Not equal are those believers who sit (at home) and receive no hurt, and those who strive and fight in the cause of God with their goods and their persons. God hath granted a grade higher to those who strive and fight with their goods and persons than to those who sit (at home). Unto all (in Faith) hath God promised good: But those who strive and fight hath He distinguished above those who sit (at home) by a special reward,

Other Suras assert that God guides all whom He wills to guide, so there is inconsistency here. For example:

9:27:   Again will God, after this, turn (in mercy) to whom He will: for God is Oft-forgiving, Most Merciful.

10:107:   If God do touch thee with hurt, there is none can remove it but He: If he do design some benefit for thee, there is none can keep back His favour: He causeth it to reach whomsoever of

His servants he pleaseth. And He is the Oft-forgiving, Most Merciful.

11:2, 3: (It teacheth) that ye should worship none but God. (Say:) 'Verily I am (Sent) unto you from Him to warn and to bring glad tidings:' (And to preach thus), 'Seek ye the forgiveness of your Lord, and turn to Him in repentance; that He may grant you enjoyment, good (and true), for a term appointed, and bestow His abounding grace on all who abound in merit! But if ye turn away, then I fear for you the Penalty of a Great Day...:

3:74: For His mercy He specially chooseth whom He pleaseth; for God is the Lord of bounties unbounded.

When we consider the doctrine of Predestination in the Koran it can be seen that the will of Allah in bestowing grace and mercy is wholly arbitrary. No Sura clearly reveals the universality of Allah's grace and mercy. In contrast to this, the Bible gives assurances of God's mercy and grace, which the universality of His Law of Love absolutely affirms.

There are many references in the Koran to Allah's love, grace and mercy, which leave the Moslem with a great dilemma. To deny that Allah loves is to deny the truth of the Koran. However, to accept that Allah does love (even though it limits His love to those who are worthy) makes Him wholly dependent on His creation for the satisfaction and reciprocation of His love.

The capacity for love in men, and in animals, proves that God does love. It proves that love is His very nature and the essence of His Being. Love in the creature infallibly proves love in the Creator.

God can only be both loving and yet independent of His creation if there is, as the Old and New Testaments clearly reveal, a Plurality of Persons within the Unity of the Godhead.

It will be necessary to consider this evidence in some detail, but first of all we shall consider the doctrines of Predestination, Salvation and the testimony of the Koran to the Scriptures.

3

Divine Sovereignty in the Koran

In this section we quote so many Suras dealing with Allah's predestinating all human actions (both good and evil) in order to show that this is the consistent teaching of the Koran. The character of Allah, tested by the Law of Love, fails the test of God's Law completely. His unconditional predestination of some to Heaven and others to Hell is completely arbitrary, (decided or arranged without any reason or plan, unfairly), excluding free will.

This predestination by Allah effectively says that sin has made no difference at all to the grounds on which He now bestows the blessings of Providence. If Divine righteousness does not need to be satisfied, then there is nothing to prevent sinners receiving these blessings in Hell itself. This theory (that divorces God's goodness and mercy from His love) is totally illogical and stands self-condemned.

6:35:   If their spurning is hard on the
          mind, yet if thou wert able to seek

a tunnel in the ground or a ladder to the skies and bring them a Sign, (What good?). If it were God's will, He could gather them together unto true guidance: So be not thou amongst those who are swayed by ignorance (and impatience)! (Note here, Mohammed was more anxious to bring men to heaven than Allah)

35:8: Is he, then, to whom the evil of his conduct is made alluring, so that he looks upon it as good, (equal to one who is rightly guided)? For God leaves to stray whom He wills, and guides who He wills. So let not thy soul go out in (vainly) sighing after them: For God knows well all that they do!

16:36, 37: For we assuredly sent amongst every People an apostle, (with the Command), 'Serve God, and eschew Evil': Of the people were some whom God guided, and some on whom Error became inevitably (established). So travel through the earth, and see what was the end of those who denied (the Truth). If thou art anxious for their guidance, yet God guideth not such as He leaves to stray, and there is none to help them.

16:93: If God so willed, He could make you all one People: But He leaves straying whom He pleases, and He guides whom He pleases: but ye shall certainly be called to account for all your actions.

11:118,119: If thy Lord had so willed, He could have made mankind one People: but they will not cease to dispute, except those on whom the Lord hath bestowed His Mercy: and for this did He create them: and the Word of thy Lord shall be fulfilled: 'I will fill Hell with Jinns and men all together.'

16:9: And unto God leads straight the Way, but there are ways that turn aside: if God had willed, He could have guided all of you.

32:13: If We had so willed, We could certainly have brought every soul its true guidance: But the Word from Me will come true, 'I will fill Hell with Jinns and men all together.'

36:7-10: The Word is proved true against the greater part of them: for they do not believe. We have put yokes round their necks right up to their chins, so that their heads are forced up (and they cannot see). And We have put a bar in front of them and a bar behind them, and further, We have covered them up; so that they cannot see. The same is it to them whether thou admonish them or thou do not admonish them: they will not believe.

39:36:   Is not God enough for His servant? But they try to frighten thee with other (gods) besides Him! For such as God leaves to stray, there can be no guide.

42:8:   If God had so willed, He could have made them a single people; but He admits whom He will to His Mercy; and the wrong-doers will have no protector nor helper.

74:31:   Thus doth God leave to stray whom He pleaseth, and guide whom He pleaseth: and none can know the forces of thy Lord, except He. And this is no other than a warning to mankind.

6:111:   Even if We did send unto them angels, and the dead did speak unto them, and We gathered together all things before their very eyes, they are not the ones to believe, unless it is in God's Plan. But most of them ignore (the truth).

6:125:   Those whom God (in His Plan) willeth to guide, He openeth their breast to Islam; those whom He willeth to leave straying, He maketh their breast close and constricted, as if they had to climb up to the skies: thus doth God (heap) the penalty on those who refuse to believe.

The predestinating of all human actions, both good and evil, is the consistent teaching of the Koran. Yet it is true that Suras Women (v81) and the Family of Imran (v80) teach free will. On the basis of these Suras many deny that the Koran teaches Predestination. But this view is not capable of being harmonised with the Predestination Suras. To say that other Suras teach free will is to say that the Koran teaches contradictory doctrines.

In his book *The Influence of Islam*, E.J. Bolus refers to the effect of this belief in Allah's all-predestinating decrees on prayer:

Both Mohammed and the Mohammedan, impressed with the idea that the will of Allah is fixed and unalterable, reject the Christian view of prayer as a communing with God, and a petitioning for spiritual and material benefits. To ask boons from Allah speaks of presumption and impertinence. To attempt to deflect one's destiny is useless rebellion. Moslem prayer substantially consists in uttering statements of belief, including ejaculations about the lofty character of Allah.

This doctrine of Predestination really denies the possibility of both good and evil, being, what Dr Fairbairn called in his book entitled *The Philosophy of the Christian Religion*, 'the Pantheism of the Divine Will.' Man, according to this theory, is not a moral being, but an automaton, a robot, for freedom of the will is necessary to morality, and responsibility. Only choosing to act according to God's Will can be good in human beings. Only choosing to disobey His will can be evil.

This type of Predestination is also a doctrine that completely destroys the Divine Unity – the basic doctrine of the Koran. It is impossible for both good and evil to spring from the same source. This is why there is the necessity for regeneration (spoken of as the new birth in the Bible), in order to enter the Kingdom of Heaven (John 3:3,5; Matt. 7:16-18; Jas. 3:13). Christ also showed the impossibility of God having two opposing natures within Himself. On being accused of casting Satan out through Satan He said:

> Every kingdom divided against itself will be ruined, and every city or household divided against itself will not stand (Matt. 12:25).

Many people choose to believe in such a Predestination, thinking that if God had granted free will to angels or humans it would mean the sacrificing of His own Sovereignty. Yet when we look to the Bible we see this is not so.

In creating man the Bible states that God created him in His own image and after His own likeness (Gen. 1:26). Man was created a moral being. A sovereign act of God bestowed free will on man, and God's sovereign acts cannot destroy His sovereignty. God is both sovereign in what He permits and what He does not permit. His sovereignty could only be compromised if a created being forced on God something He had not ordained to allow, so that He had no choice in the matter.

Free will in human beings and in celestial beings was absolutely necessary if God was to receive the highest possible kind of glory from created beings – moral glory. God receives the glory of obedience that is prompted by love, and which is great enough to conquer any temptation to disobedience. As we have previously stated, there is no virtue in untested obedience. Therefore to deny human free will robs God of the possibility of His receiving any higher kind of obedience. What He would be receiving would be no more than the mechanical 'obedience' of a plant that grows towards the light.

As we have already stated, in order to be able to love, one has to have freedom of choice, yet this also brings with it the possibility of evil. However, this allowance of evil is still better (in this sense only) than that God should never be able to receive the highest form of glory possible to Him as Almighty Creator. This is especially so since

He has ordained to overrule the evil that He has permitted (through allowing free-will) through sending His own Son to become a Redeemer for all who put their trust in His saving work.

In natural realms the harvest of a crop is always according to the seed that has been sown. The same can be said of the spiritual realm. God loves the sinner, but hates the sin. Our sins were judged in Christ, and placing our trust in Him saves us from judgement. But when sinners reject Christ in unbelief, there can be no forgiveness of sin. Unbelief makes repentance impossible and therefore reconciliation to God impossible. Those who do not believe will live eternally with the consequences of their sin. The consequences of our actions are eternally fixed by the righteousness of God.

4

The Doctrine of Salvation in the Koran

On every point the Koran fails to stand the test which the Laws of God supply. The doctrine of salvation in the Koran makes God both unjust and unmerciful. It completely contradicts all the Suras that speak of Allah's mercy and justice, and the Koranic doctrine of Allah's predestination of both good and evil makes his judgement upon himself only. Think about it! If Allah has already predetermined every single action there can be no moral judgement. The individual cannot be held responsible where he or she has no free will in the first place.

The Koranic doctrine of salvation sacrifices both justice and mercy. It is also illogical, because it makes salvation (that has already been predestined!) dependant on adding good deeds to belief in Allah. Good deeds are said to outweigh the evil deeds, yet in this there is no room for mercy.

No country in the world allows the keeping of

some laws to balance out and pay for the breaking of other laws. In fact this idea could very well encourage people to break the law in 'moderate ways'. After all, if I go and break one law, I can just go and do something good and then there is no penalty to pay. No country in the world functions in this way, yet we are supposed to believe that a perfect and Holy God does.

Another point to be considered is this: since the Koran states that we are already predestined to Heaven or Hell, then even if I do good works it ultimately makes no difference. My good works may 'balance' out the bad I have done; yet Allah has already decided my fate anyway!

It is impossible for any sinner to live in perfect obedience to the Law of Love. We are flawed beings, and can never offer perfect works, let alone perfect love. We are totally incapable of meeting the claims of God's law. Yet God, as revealed in the Bible, is loving and merciful. He provided a Saviour who could bear for us the condemnation of His Law by the infinite merits of His sacrifice. This Saviour was (as true, sinless, representative man) the only one who could live this life of perfect love to God. He underwent many harsh tests, which revealed His perfection. Through His saving work He secured (for believers) the perfect righteousness which is the condition of Eternal Life.

Evidence of the Koran's Inadequacy

The inadequacy of the God of the Koran to meet the spiritual need of Moslems is well attested by the fact that some Moslems (especially among the mystics) speak of Mohammed as an intercessor for them. Yet the Koran states that he is only one who warns (Sura 88:21-22). The Sufis of Persia (Iran), the Dervishies with their mystic prayer dance, and the Sennousi of North Africa with their sacred brotherhoods, show how wide such mysticism is.

Another indication of the inadequacy of the Koran to meet spiritual needs is seen in the words of a Moslem girl to the editor of a Moslem newspaper in Lahore.

> 'I am a girl of 20, and from the age of twelve I have done every sin you can think of…. Alas! There is nothing left for me but Hell when I ask you sincerely, what am I to do to be saved?… I have been told to repent, but the truth is, I cannot repent, as what I have done, I have enjoyed doing, although it was sin. How will you advise me what to do so as to be saved from Hell?'

To this poor girl the Moslem editor could only reply:

> 'Turn over a new leaf; lead a righteous life henceforth. This alone will wash away past sins. This is the only true atonement. Sins are washed off, the Koran assures us, by good deeds, and by these alone.'

Due to our sinful nature we often find that the things we know to be wrong are still attractive to us, and, as in the case above, fear of Hell does not necessarily produce repentance. If only this young Muslim girl could have been told of the Saviour. She would see the perfect One who loves her, and find that, in the light of His revelation, her life of sin was not so attractive. It is only Jesus' purity and the light of His love that really enable us see how wrong our sinful actions are. Those who come to God through Christ have willingly turned from sin to a living Saviour, their previous sin no longer appearing attractive in any way.

Sir Monier-Willimas, the great Orientalist, formerly Boden Professor of Sanskrit in Oxford University, who spent forty-two years studying the religious books of the East, said, on comparing them with the religion of the Bible:

'Pile them, if you will, on the left side of your study table; but place your own Bible on the right side, all by itself, all alone – and with a wide gap between.'

The test of Divine law will reveal how immeasurably wide this gap is. Christ claimed that the whole purpose of His coming into the world was to fulfil the Law's demands upon us. No other religion in the world even understands what the requirements of God's laws are.

Do not think that I have come to abolish the Law or the Prophets; I have not come to abolish them but to fulfil them (Matt. 5:17).

5

Was Jesus Crucified?

According to many Muslims Jesus was not crucified on the cross. Instead, Allah is supposed to have cast the likeness of Jesus on Judas whom the Jews then crucified. They reach this conclusion from the following Surah:

> 'That they said (in boast); "We killed Christ Jesus the son of Mary, the Apostle of God'; but they killed him not, nor crucified him, but so it was made to appear to them, and those who differ theirein are full of doubts, with no (certain) knowledge but only conjecture to follow, for of a surety they killed him not: Nay, God raised him up unto Himself; and God is Exalted in Power, Wise;' (Surah 4:157-158).

Mohammed would have been aware that Christians believed that Christ had been crucified, bearing God's judgement on man's sin. However, he chose to believe the apocryphal book 'The Acts of John' which denies the Christian doctrine of salvation.

No Christian accepts 'The Acts of John' as part of the Bible. 'The Acts of John' makes Jesus say to John:

> 'Unto the multitude in Jerusalem, I am being crucified and pierced with lances, and gall and vinegar is being given me to drink. But now I speak unto thee.... Neither am I he who is on the cross whom thou now seest, but only hearest a voice. I was reckoned to be that which I am not, not being what I am to others.... Nothing therefore of the things which they will say of me have I suffered. (Quoted by Sweetman, *Islam and Christianity,* pp. 97, 99, 101)

The 'Acts of John' (from where Mohammed gained information) state that Jesus was not crucified and that he remained in Jerusalem and spoke to John. This does not suit Mohammed and so he states that Allah took Jesus to heaven!

In the light of all this there is an important point we have to consider. Surely it is totally illogical that whilst Moslems are encouraged not to trust any man who claimed to be a deceiver, they choose to believe in Allah, who is (according to the Koran) a self-confessed deceiver?

Nothing can be more certain than that the man whom the Jews crucified as Jesus was the same man they arrested in the garden of Gethsemane.

1. When arrested in the garden this man said: 'Judas, are you betraying the Son of Man with a kiss?' (Luke 22:48).

2. To those who were sent to arrest him he said: 'Every day I was with you in the temple courts, and you did not lay a hand on me. But this is your hour – when darkness reigns' (Luke 22:53).

3. Peter wanted to defend Jesus and cut off the right ear of Malchus, a servant of the High Priest. Jesus healed Him, saying to Peter: 'Put your sword back in its place, for all who draw the sword will die by the sword. Do you think I cannot call on my Father, and he will at once put at my disposal more than twelve legions of angels? But how then would the Scriptures be fulfilled that say it must happen in this way?' (Matt. 26:51-54; Mark 14:43-50; Luke 22:47-53; John 18:1-11). If Malchus had not been healed by Jesus, the Gospel record would certainly have been contradicted, but it never was.

4. At the trial of this man before the Sanhedrin, witnesses stood up and spoke against him with the words: 'We heard him say, "I will destroy this man-made temple and in three days will build another, not made by man"' (Mark 14:58). Jesus did not deny it.

5. When the High Priest said to him: 'Are you Christ, the Son of the Blessed One?' 'I am,' said Jesus. 'And you will see the Son of Man sitting at the right hand of the Mighty One and coming on the clouds of heaven' (Mark 14:61-62).

6. When Pilate said: 'You are a King, then!' Jesus replied: 'You are right in saying I am a king. In fact, for this reason I was born, and for this I came into the world, to testify to the truth. Everyone on the side of truth listens to me' (John 18:37).

7. On the cross this man prayed for those who crucified him: 'Father, forgive them, for they do not know what they are doing' (Luke 23:34). Logically speaking, if this person was another man with the likeness of Jesus he would be shouting out that he was innocent, and that they were crucifying the wrong man!

8. The usual way in which the Jews would execute the death penalty would be by stoning. This was impossible since they were under Roman law, which would not allow this. Therefore the scriptures in the Old Testament, which stated that Jesus would be crucified (Ps. 22, Zech. 12:10) revealed that the Jewish nation would be under the dominion of Rome a thousand years before it took place.

9. When the believing thief said to this man, 'Jesus, remember me when you come into your kingdom,' this man answered: 'I tell you the truth, today you will be with me in paradise' (Luke 23:42-43). Any man suddenly finding himself in such a position would certainly not be willing, or even capable of reaching out to others. He would be shouting out for justice and going

through great mental turmoil, not comforting a thief! It is totally illogical to believe that another man was crucified in the place of Jesus!

Christ's personal predictions of His death and resurrection also present evidence that it was Jesus Himself, and not some other man, who was crucified as Jesus (Matt. 17:1-9; 20:17-28; 21:33-44; 26:6-12,21-32, 36-42, 55, 63-65).

When we look at the character of Jesus in the Gospels we find a person who lived in perfect harmony with God. He had no time for the lies and deceiving ways of religious leaders who sought to trap Him with their questions. When Jesus said that He would heal the sick, they were healed. When Jesus said that He would raise the dead they were raised. When He predicted His death and resurrection He did so as one with a faultless record. Why then should we doubt Him?

Muslims continue to believe that Allah saved Jesus by causing another man to bear the sentence of condemnation. Therefore they cannot logically object to the Biblical doctrine, which states that God saved sinners by Christ's substitution!

God commands us to love Him with all of our heart, and to love our neighbour as ourselves. It would have been both hypocritical and immoral for God to have deliberately caused another to suffer a judgement which Jesus had specifically come to take upon Himself.

Another point, which Mohammed failed to

consider, is the all-important question: Why would the Jews insist on the crucifixion of Jesus (despite Pilate trying to prevent it) if Jesus were only a prophet?

The Jews wanted to put Jesus to death because of His claims to Deity. In their minds this was blasphemy, and warranted the death penalty. When Pilate said: 'I find no basis for a charge against him', the Jews insisted: 'We have a law, and according to that law he must die, because he claimed to be the Son of God' (John 19:7).

When the Gospels were published the Jews did not contradict the biblical record, which clearly states that they demanded Christ's crucifixion on the grounds of blasphemy. Moslems denied that He made this claim, yet unbelievers living at the time of Christ give irrefutable proof that Jesus had done so. Their Law against false witness made it impossible for the Jews to bring a charge of blasphemy against Jesus unless they had heard him claim to be the Son of God. That is why the High Priest asked: 'Are you the Son of God?' at the trial of Jesus.

No imperfect being could ever pay the perfect price for man's sin, or reconcile man to God. Only divine substitution could reveal the infinite greatness of God's love to sinners, and do everything that divine love could do in order to win the love of a sinner's heart.

'God was reconciling the world to himself in Christ, not counting men's sins against them...

God made him who had no sin to be sin for us, so that in him we might become the righteousness of God' (2 Cor. 5:19, 21).

'He himself bore our sins in his body on the tree, so that we might die to sins and live for righteousness; by his wounds you have been healed' (2 Pet. 2:24).

'For God so loved the world that he gave his one and only Son, that whoever believes in him shall not perish but have eternal life' (John 3:16).

6

The Rejection of Christ as Saviour

The Koran states that forgiveness of sin depends on so-called 'good deeds' that outweigh evil deeds. This denies the Biblical doctrine, which states that salvation depends on faith in Christ. It is only Jesus who has satisfied the twofold claims of the law – both precept and penalty, on our behalf.

The following three Suras will be of interest to us. The first states that none will be helped on the Day of Judgement. Yet the second and third show that angels will intercede for people. This is rather strange: surely stating that salvation depends entirely on good deeds outweighing bad deeds excludes all intercession?

2.48:   Then guard yourselves against a day when one shall not avail another nor shall intercession be accepted for her, nor shall compensation be taken from her, nor shall anyone be helped (from outside).

40:7:   Those who sustain the Throne (of

God) and those around it sing Glory and Praise to their Lord; believe in Him; and implore Forgiveness for those who believe: 'Our Lord! Thy reach is over all things, in Mercy and Knowledge. Forgive, then, those who turn in Repentance, and follow Thy Path; and preserve them from the Penalty of the Blazing Fire!'

42:5: The heavens are almost rent assunder from above them (by His Glory): and the angels celebrate the Praises of their Lord, and pray for forgiveness for (all) beings on earth: Behold! Verily God is He, the Oft-Forgiving, Most Merciful.

Mohammed says that any contradiction in the Koran would disprove its divine origin.

Substitution – the Highest Expression of Love
Human love has often been expressed by a person bearing another's punishment, even if this meant death. An example of this substitution is found in Schamyl, a great Circassian leader.

Schamyl (a Moslem) championed his people's cause and liberty. For over thirty years he held up the advance of Russia in the Caucasus, finally dying in 1871. At one period of his rule, bribery and corruption was so rife that he needed to take harsh measures to eliminate it. One hundred lashes would be given to anyone found guilty of any of the above crimes. Shortly after this decree, his own mother was found guilty.

Schamyl shut himself away in a tent and fasted for two days. If he made an exception for his mother he would no longer be seen as either a just lawgiver, or man of his word. But how could he have his mother lashed? His love for his mother could hardly be reconciled with the execution of the sentence that his justice as lawgiver demanded. Schamyl eventually found the solution. After his mother had been whipped five times he called a halt to the whipping. He then received the remaining ninety-five lashes.

Another example of substitution is as follows:

The Greek King of Locris made the loss of two eyes the penalty for breaking one of his laws. His own son was brought before him as the first offender. He upheld the authority of his law, yet at the same time exercised mercy. He had one of his own eyes put out to save his son from becoming blind. Throughout all history we find amazing stories of sacrifice.

After the Second World War there were many stories told of men and women who sacrificed their lives for others in the prison camps. One noted occasion occurred when men were selected to die by starvation because another prisoner had escaped. Among those selected was a Polish soldier named Gajowniczek who cried out: 'My wife! My poor children!' As the guards prepared to march off the doomed men, a Roman Catholic priest stepped forward and said he wanted to take the place of Gajowniczek. The German officer thought he was mad, but granted his request. So the priest died that another might live.

In order to receive God's love man needs to repent of sin and desire true righteousness.

He can find neither true repentance nor true righteousness within himself. All his efforts and good works are already flawed. He is an imperfect being, and his idea of righteousness falls far below the demands of the Holy One.

It is only the death of Christ that secures both adequate repentance and righteousness. The cross shows both the righteousness and love of God. It shows man just how much God hates sin, and also reveals how much God loves man. A substitute dies in our place, so that we can receive His righteousness as our own. This substitute willingly gave His own life. Today, many millions seeing what God did at Calvary, have been brought to repentance. In seeing true holiness and love men and women have become aware of their sin and need of salvation. They understand true righteousness, and through Christ's gift of life, they can claim it as their own.

God cannot by-pass our evil ways and treat us as dear and loyal children without making sin to appear trivial. He will not set aside His law of righteousness. Forgiveness can come only through a medium that safeguards righteousness. The substitution of Christ's death for our punishment answers this purpose. It more effectually binds us to God and righteousness than our own punishment would have done. It is not our suffering that God desires. What He desires is a permanent establishment in holiness, which unites us to Him. The two great ends of punishment (homage to law and reformation of the law-breaker) are both secured by the death of Christ.

The death of Christ, then, has made forgiveness possible, because it enables men to repent with an adequate repentance, and because it magnifies righteousness and binds men to God.

7

The Testimony of the Koran to the Scriptures

Moslems believe that the Christian scriptures are not the same as they were in the time of Mohammed. They believe scripture has been altered to present Christ as Deity Incarnate in the virgin-born son of Mary, and then being seen as the Saviour of the world by His sacrifice at Calvary. Moslems also believe that scripture was altered to get rid of their testimony to Mohammed as the Prophet like unto Moses (Deut. 18:15, 18) and the promised Paraclete (John 14:16).

Moslems believe that the Koran teaches that not only has this alteration taken place, but that, as final revelation, the Koran has abrogated both the Old and New Testaments. Therefore, it is necessary to show Moslems that the Koran itself teaches no such doctrines.

In his book, *The Koran*, Sir William Muir gives the Arabic text and English translation of every Sura in the Koran which refers to the Scriptures and also to abrogation. We give the following summary:

1. The Koran declares that God Himself gave the Scriptures to the prophets and to Jesus:

   a. 'We did give the Book Taurat (the Law) to Moses' (Sura 32:23,cf 2:53; 11:17; 21:25; 25:35; 37:117; 40:53). The Pentateuch is clearly intended.
   b. 'To David we gave the Zabur' (Psalms) – (Sura 17:55)
   c. 'We gave Him (Jesus) the Injil' (Evangel) – (Suras 5:49;19:30; 57:27).
   d. That 'He sent down the Taurat and the Injil for the guidance of mankind' (Sura:3:3).

2. The Scriptures are spoken of in terms of high praise. Thus the Taurat is said to be:

   a. 'The Book of God' (5:47; cf. 2:93; 3:23).
   b. 'The Word of God' (2:75)
   c. 'Al Furquan', i.e. The illumination (21:50), a title of distinction also given to the Koran.
   d. 'The Perspicuous' (or Enlightening Book), (Sura 3:184). Jalaludin in his commentary says that the Taurat and the Injil are meant here.
   e. 'A light and a guidance to men ... complete to him who acts aright' (6:91; 155).

3. Other passages refer to the inspiration, authority and proper use of the Scriptures in possession of 'the people of the Book.' Thus:

a. 'We have sent thee (Mohammed) inspiration, as We sent it to Noah and the Messengers after him (4:163, cf. 21:7; 42:1-3; 3:44).

b. 'They (the Jews) have inherited the Book' (7:169, cf. 42:14).

c. 'They already have the Taurat in which is God's judgement' (5:44).

d. Jews and Christians are said to be diligent readers of their scriptures (10:94, cf. 3:110).

e. Jews who hold fast by the Book will be rewarded (7:170), so too, if they (the Jews and Christians) observe the Taurat and Injil (5:68-69).

f. Mohammed himself is called to believe in the Scriptures and declares his unqualified faith in them: 'but say: "I believe in the Book which God has sent down..." (42:15; 29:46; 3:78). Also, "If thou wert in doubt as to what We have revealed unto thee, then ask those who have been reading the Book from before thee: the Truth hath indeed come to thee from thy Lord: so be in no wise of those in doubt"' (10:94).

g. The Jews who rejected the Injil (gospel) are most severely condemned for saying, 'We believe in some but reject others' (4:150-151).

Finally, it is stated that the Koran verifies and attests the previous scriptures:

Sura 3:3:   It is He who sent down to thee (step by step), in truth, the Book, confirming what went before it; and He sent down the Law (of Moses) and the Gospel (of Jesus) before this, as a guide to mankind, and He sent down the Criterion (of judgement between right and wrong).

See also Suras 10:37; 45:16-17; 6:92; 2:41, 87, 91, 99.

We also find that Suras 18:27; 10:64; 6:34, 115 all state that the Word of God cannot be altered or changed. Sura 18:27 says:

'And recite (and teach) what has been revealed to thee of the Book of thy Lord: none can change His Words, and none wilt thou find as a refuge other than Him.

The fact that Mohammed made so many references to scriptures (Old and New Testament) shows that he did not regard them as having been corrupted or abrogated by the Koran. To 'verify,' 'attest,' and 'confirm,' completely excludes both corruption and abrogation.

It is obvious that Mohammed did not regard the Scriptures as either corrupted in his day, or as abrogated by the Koran. Mohammed never brought any charges (concerning corrupting the scriptures) against the Christians. There were never any accusations that scripture had been changed to present a different Christ from that which the Koran presents to us. The testimony of Mohammed himself shows us how we are to interpret his words in Sura 2: 40-43:

> 'O children of Israel! Call to mind the (special) favour which I bestowed upon you, and fulfil your Covenant with Me as I fulfil My Covenant with you, and fear none but Me. And believe in what I reveal, confirming the revelation which is with you, and be not the first to reject faith therein, nor sell My Signs for a small price; and fear Me, and Me alone. And cover not Truth with falsehood, nor conceal the Truth when ye know (what it is).'

Later, in the same Sura, we read:

> 'Can ye (O ye men of Faith) entertain the hope that they will believe in you? – Seeing that a party of them heard the Word of God, and perverted it knowingly after they understood it' (Sura 2:75).

The above Sura does not say that the word of God was altered. What Mohammed is referring to is the Jewish interpretation of scripture. They did not agree with his belief that Deuteronomy 18:15,18 spoke of him. He saw this as false interpretation and therefore perversion. It cannot be a charge of perverting the scriptures, since he appeals to scripture as bearing witness to him!

Moslems state that the scriptures were altered after the time when Mohammed declared that the Koran was sent to 'attest,' 'verify,' and 'confirm' them. This is used to justify their belief that the scripture testimony to Christ has been altered. Yet this is to completely ignore a very important fact:

When we compare present day scriptures with early biblical manuscripts that date long before the time of Mohammed, it can be clearly seen that our scriptures are the same as those in use at the time of Mohammed. The biblical doctrines of God, Christ, the Holy Spirit and salvation are exactly the same, and there is no record of Mohammed within the Bible. Evidence that there has been no change to scripture totally destroys the foundations of Islam, proving the Koran to be both unnecessary and false. Let us now look at some of the evidence:

Evidence Concerning the New Testament
We now have more than 5,300 Greek manuscripts of the New Testament for comparison with our present New Testament.

1. Codex Vaticanus (AD 325–350), preserved in the Vatican Library and containing nearly the whole Bible.
2. Codex Sinaiticus (AD 350), now in the British Museum. It contains nearly all the New Testament, and over half the Old Testament.
3. Codex Alexandrinus (AD 400), also in the British Museum, containing almost the whole Bible.

4. Codex Ephraemi (5th century) located in the Bibliotheque Nationale, Paris. Containing the whole of the New Testament apart from 2 Thessalonians and 2 John.

5. Codex Bezae (ca. 450) in the Cambridge University Library. It contains the Gospels and Acts in both Greek and Latin.

6. Codex Washingtonensis (ca.450) contains the four Gospels.

7. Codex Claromontanus (6th century), contains Paul's Letters in Greek and Latin.

8. The Chester Beatty Papyri (AD 200) in Dublin University, and owned in part by the University of Michigan. Three of these papyrus codices contain large portions of the New Testament.

9. Bodmer Papyrus 11 (ca. 150–200), 'the most important discovery of N.T. manuscripts since the purchase of the Chester Beatty Papyri.'

All these documents teach the same doctrines as our Gospels and New Testament.

The Versions
Translations of the New Testament were made circa AD 150 in Syriac and Latin. They bring us very near to the time of the originals.

1. The old Syriac version (the name given to the Christian Aramaic, written in a distinctive form of the Aramaic alphabet).

2. The Peshita Syriac was the standard version

produced between AD 150-250. More than 350 extant manuscripts of this version exist dating from the fifth century.

3. The Palestinian Syriac, dated between AD 400–500. It is recorded that Polycarp (disciple of the Apostle John) translated the New Testament into Syriac for Phioloxenas, Bishop of Mabug.

4. Old Latin versions. Testimonies show this version was in circulation in the third century.

5. African Old Latin – Codex Rabbiensis – which E. A. Lowe says 'shows paleographical marks of having been copied from a second century papyrus'.

6. Codex Corbiensis (AD 400–500) contains the four Gospels.

7. Codex Vercellensis (AD 360).

8. Codex Palatinus (5th century AD).

9. Latin Vulgate translated by Jerome, secretary of Damasus, Bishop of Rome, at his request between 364 and 384 AD.

10. Coptic or Egyptian versions. Believed to have been translated between 200–300 AD.

11. The Sahidic, dated the beginning of the 3rd century.

12. The Boharic (Ca. 4th century).

13. Middle Egyptian (4th–5th centuries).

14. Armenian (400 AD).

15. Gothic (4th century)

16. Georgian (5th century)

17. Ethiopic (6th century).

18. Nubian (6th century).

All these versions were in circulation before Mohammed was born. They clearly reveal that the doctrines of our present Gospels have not been changed. None make any reference to Mohammed.

The Evidence of Quotations

There are many quotations of the New Testament by early Christian writers (the Church Fathers). Putting them all together, along with quotations of the New Testament by those who opposed it, gives us a record of the whole of the New Testament, with only a few verses not quoted. From viewing them one clearly sees that the New Testament scriptures we have today are the same as those in the first centuries after Christ.

Justyn Martyr (circa AD 114) made 330 quotations from the New Testament, whilst Ireneaus (circa AD 120–202) made 1,819; Clement of Alexandria 2,406; Origon 17,992; Tertullian 7,258; Hippolytus 1,378 and Eusebius 5,176. This gives us 36,289 quotations in all.

Professor Norman Geisler in his book, *Christian Apologetics* (pp. 307-308), states that that the total count of early Greek manuscripts of the New Testament is now around 5,000 with a 99%+ accuracy. The average gap between the original composition and earliest copy is over 1,000 years for other books. Yet the New Testament has a fragment within one generation from its original composition, and whole books within about 100 years from the time of the autograph, and the entire New Testament within 250 years.

There is a large index of citations by the Church Fathers of antiquity in the British Museum. It was compiled by Dean Burgon and consists of sixteen thick volumes containing 86,489 quotations.

The Old Testament – Evidences of Unchanged Doctrines

Until the discovery of the Dead Sea Scrolls the oldest Hebrew Old Testament manuscript was dated about AD 900. This is because the Jews destroyed old copies when new ones had been completed. Deists assumed that, since they were copied by hand, many errors must have crept in, thus making unreliable translations. They expect us to believe that God brought about the scriptures through supernatural Divine Revelation, but was then not bothered to make sure they remained accurate. Looking at the Dead Sea Scrolls, which contain many portions of the Old Testament, one finds no differences (when comparing with modern translations) in the text concerning any of the doctrines of the Christian faith. Through the period of about 1,300 years separating these scrolls from the earliest previously known manuscripts, the all-wise God marvellously preserved His revelation through the Old Testament prophets, of whom Adam was the first (Acts 3:21).

The Talmudists (AD 100–500)
Josh McDowell quotes Samuel Davidson:

> 'An authentic copy must be the exemplar, from which the transcriber ought not in the least to deviate from. No word or letter, not even a yod, must be written from memory, the scribe not having looked at the codex before him. Between every consonant the space of a hair or a thread must intervene. Between every new parasahah, or section, the breadth of nine consonants; between every book three lines. The fifth book of Moses must terminate exactly with a line; but the rest need not do so.

McDowell quotes Sir F. Kenyon, in *Our Bible and the Ancient Manuscripts*, on the same subject:

> The extreme care, which was devoted to the transcription of manuscripts, explains the disappearance of earlier copies. When a manuscript had been copied with the exactitude prescribed by a Talmud, and had been duly verified, it was accepted as authentic, and regarded as being equal with any other copy. If all were equally correct, age gave no advantage to a manuscript; on the contrary, age was a positive disadvantage, since a manuscript was liable to become defaced or damaged with the lapse of time. A damaged or imperfect copy was at once condemned as unfit for use.

The Massoretic Period (AD 500–900)

Up until this period in time the Hebrew text was purely consonantal. Jewish Hebrew scholars felt this to be a disadvantage where pronunciation was concerned. They undertook to supply vowel points to the text, which was then known as the 'Massoretic' text. It is accepted as the standard Hebrew text today.

> 'The Massorettes were well-disciplined, and treated the text with great reverence. They devised a complicated system of safeguards against possible scribal errors. For example, they counted the number of times each letter occurs in each book. "Everything countable seems to have been counted," says Wheeler Robinson. The Massorettes also made up mnemonics by which the various totals might be readily remembered. Besides recording varieties of reading, tradition or conjecture, the Massorettes undertook a number of calculations that did not enter into the ordinary sphere of textual criticism.
>
> They numbered the verses, words, and letters of every book. They calculated the middle word and middle letter of each. They enumerated verses, which contained all the letters of the alphabet, or a certain number of them; and so on. These trivialities, as we may rightly consider them, had yet the effect of securing minute attention to the precise transmission of the text; and they are but an excessive manifestation of a respect for the sacred scriptures, which in itself

deserves nothing but praise. The Massorettes were indeed anxious that not one jot or tittle, not one smallest letter, nor any tiny part of a letter, of the Law should pass away or be lost' (Josh McDowell, *Evidence Which Demands a Verdict, pp. 54-55*).

The Historical Accuracy of the Old Testament
Dr. R. D. Wilson wrote *The Scientific Investigation of the Old Testament*. Speaking to the Bible League in the 1920s he said:

For forty-five years since I left college, I devoted myself continuously to the one great study of the Old Testament in all its languages, and in all its archaeology, in all its translations, and as far as possible, everything bearing on its text and history. The result of my forty-five year study has led me all the time to a firmer faith that in the Old Testament we have a true historical account of the history of the people of Israel.

After I had learned the language (to which he had devoted fifteen years of study), I got to work on every consonant in the Old Testament Hebrew. There are about one million and a quarter consonants, and it took me many years to read the Old Testament through and look at every consonant in it, and gather the variations found in manuscripts or in the notes of the Massorettes. I also looked at versions, parallel passages, or in the conjectural emendations of the critics, and classified them, putting them in form for use. I prize textual criticism very highly. (This occupied another fifteen years of study.)

So this is the fundamental thing I am talking about today. The result of those thirty years which I have been putting on the text has been this: There is not a page of the Old Testament (1,390 in the Old Testament Hebrew Bible), that you can read without being sure that you can depend on the contents of the page. You can be absolutely certain that we have the text of the Old Testament that Christ and the apostles had, which has been in existence since the beginning.

I remember when it was considered very unprofitable to read over those long genealogies in the first chapters of 1st Chronicles – nine chapters of proper names, and we wondered why they were in the Bible. Today, in scientific criticism of the Old Testament, the proper names are the most necessary factor to consider.

Now, there are twenty-nine kings whose names are mentioned not only in the Old Testament, but in other documents written in their own time, and many of them under the supervision of the kings themselves: written in Egyptian, Assyrian, Persian, and on monuments and other documents which have come from the times of the kings themselves. There are 195 consonants in these 29 proper names. We find that in the documents of the Hebrew Bible, of these consonants there are only two or three about which there would be any question of their being written in exactly the same way that they are written on their own monuments by the men themselves, or under their direction some 4,000 years ago, and some about 2,400 years ago. Think of names handed down for 2,400 to 4,000 years, so that every letter is clear and correct – that is a wonder!

The Internal Witness of the Old Testament

Reading through the Old Testament we find that the religion that it speaks of is inward, belonging to the mind and heart. Love, joy, faith and hope are spoken of, as is salvation through the grace of God alone. So how do we account for this religion? The prophets say that it came from God. There is no other theory of its origin that can account for its results, its superiority and its influence.

There are critics who believe that these prophets only spoke the ideas of their time. Yet this criticism does not adequately explain how it was that this information came from sheepfolds and dungeons, from captives and shepherd kings. It did not arise from such places as the temples of Babylon, or from Delphi and Rome.

The prophets who spoke God's word, did not speak as men of their own time. They spoke of the one who knows the end from the beginning, and has all power in heaven and on earth. Neither the shackles of time nor circumstance can bind the revelation of God's will.

The Evidence of the Dead Sea Scrolls

Until the Dead Sea Scrolls were discovered in 1947 the oldest extant Hebrew manuscripts of the Old Testament dated from AD 900. Among these scrolls were two copies of Isaiah dating a thousand years before the previous earliest manuscripts. They reveal word for word accuracy in more than 95% of the Hebrew Bible. The 5% of variation consisted of obvious slips of the pen and various spellings. Dead Sea Scroll fragments of Deuteronomy and Samuel point to a different manuscript family than that of our Hebrew text. Yet they do not indicate any difference in doctrine or teaching. They do not affect the message of revelation in any way.

The Evidence of the Septuagint (LXX)

Due to the conquests of Alexander the Great, the Greek language (as spoken by ordinary people) became what English is to our own day. History also reveals that the Jews were widely dispersed at this time, and a colony ended up in Alexandria. Ptolemy had great interest in literature and was favourable to the Jews. All these factors resulted in the Hebrew Scriptures being translated into Greek, circa 285–246 BC.

Josh McDowell writes:

> The LXX being very close to the Massoretic text (AD 916) we have today, helps to establish its reliability of transmission through 1,300 years. The greatest divergence of the LXX from the Massoretic text is Jeremiah.

But archaeology has produced an abundance of evidence to substantiate the correctness of the Massoretic text. Bernard Ramm writes of the Jeremiah Seal:

> The Jeremiah Seal, a seal used to stamp the bitumen seals of wine jars, and dated from the first or second century AD, has Jeremiah 48:11 stamped on it. This seal attests the accuracy with which the text was transmitted between the time when the seal was made and the time when the manuscript was written. Furthermore, the Roberts Papyrus, which dates to the second century BC, and the Nash Papyrus, dated by Albright before 100 BC, confirm the Massoretic text.

The Targums
The Targums are Aramaic paraphrases of the Hebrew Scriptures. They were made necessary because Aramaic had taken the place of Hebrew as the language of the Jews, after their return from exile in Babylon. Present copies date from about 500 AD.

Anderson, in *The Bible, the Word of God*, says:

> The great utility of the earlier Targums consists in their vindicating the genuineness of the Hebrew text, by proving it was the same at the period that the Targums were made, as it exists among us in the present day.

75

The chief Targums are the Targums of Onkelos (60 BC) which contains the Hebrew text of the Pentateuch and the Targum of Jonathon Ben Uzziel (circa 30 BC) which contains the historical books and the Prophets.

The Mishna (AD 200)
This contains a collection of Jewish traditions and expositions of Oral Law, written in Hebrew and often regarded as the 'Second Law'. As shall be seen later, it also contains an important reference to the Gospels. The scriptural quotations are very similar to the Massoretic text, and witness to its reliability.

The Gemaras (Palestinian AD 200)
These commentaries, written in Aramaic, that grew up around the Mishna, contribute to the reliability of the Massoretic text.

The Midrash
This was made up of doctrinal studies of the Old Testament Hebrew Text.

As can be seen, there are vast amounts of material available for comparing our present day scriptures with those in existence in Mohammed's day.

The Testimony of the Creeds
Apart from the testimony of the Apostolic Fathers, who do not see Christ as a created being, we also have the Creeds. The church creeds show us the

belief of the early church, having being written to refute the rationalists of the day.

G. P. Fisher, in *The History of the Church*, writes:

The Nicene Creed, as framed in AD 325 in Nicea, enlarged in 381 at Constantinople, and among the Latins, at the Spanish Council of Toledo, reads in English as follows:

I believe in one God the Father Almighty; Maker of heaven and earth, and of all things visible and invisible. And in one Lord Jesus Christ, the only-begotten Son of God, begotten of the Father, before all worlds (God of God), Light of Light, very God of very God, begotten, not made, being of one substance (essence) with the Father; by whom all things were made; who for us men and for our salvation, came down from heaven, and was incarnate of the Holy Ghost by the Virgin Mary, and was made man; and was crucified also for us under Pontius Pilate; he suffered, and was buried; and the third day rose again according to the scriptures; and ascended into heaven, and sits at the right hand of the Father; and He shall come again with glory, to judge both the quick and the dead; whose kingdom shall have no end. And (I believe) in the Holy Ghost, the Lord and Giver of Life; who proceeds from the Father (and the Son); who with the Father and the Son together is worshipped and glorified; who spoke by the prophets.

The Council of Chalcedon in 451 also affirmed that Jesus Christ is God Incarnate.

The Doctrine of Abrogation
(To 'abrogate' means 'to do away with, to set aside')

Moslems believe that references to abrogation in the Koran refer to the Bible, with a few exceptions. However Mohammed has said that the Koran was sent to confirm the Bible, which is the complete opposite of abrogation. In believing the references in the Koran to abrogation relate to the scriptures, Mohammed is made guilty of contradiction!

Dr Pfander, in his book *The Balance of Truth* writes:

> 'The verb "nasakha", with the sense of "to abrogate," occurs only twice in the Koran and in neither of these instances is it used with reference to any part of the Old or New Testaments. On the contrary, it is used of the abrogation of certain verses of the Koran itself, of which, one Moslem commentator says, about 225 verses have been abrogated. Sura 2:106 (in the translation we have been using throughout) reads: "None of our revelations do we abrogate or cause to be forgotten, but we substitute something better or similar: Knowest thou not that God hath power over all things?" However in comparing this with another translation, we gain a clearer picture:
>
> Sura 2:106: Whatever communications we abrogate or cause to be forgotten, we bring one

better than it or like it. Do you now know that Allah has power over all things?'

'The Quran', translated by M. H. Shakir and distributed by the Al-Khoei Benevolent Foundation. (From this it appears that Allah is said to cause Mohammed to forget his word).

Dr Pfander also refers to a Muslim commentator who denies that the Koran abrogates the Bible. Shaik Haja Rahmatu'llah of Delhi, in his Isharu'l Raqq (pp. 11-12), says that the statement that the Law (Taurat) was abrogated by the Zabur (Psalms), and the Zabur by the appearance of the Injil (Gospel), is a falsehood of which there is no trace in the Koran.

In conclusion we again note that there is irrefutable evidence that the present day scriptures of both Old and New Testaments are the same doctrinally as those which Mohammed asserts the Koran was sent to confirm. To confirm means that the Koran can never have abrogated these scriptures.

8

Mohammed's Claim
to be Christ's Successor

Mohammed claimed to be the Person referred to by Christ in John 14:16. The Greek word translated 'Comforter' in this verse is *parakletos*, meaning 'one called alongside to help'. It is translated 'advocate' in 1 John 2:1.

> Sura 61:6 reads: And remember, Jesus, the son of Mary, said: 'O children of Israel! I am the apostle of God (sent) to you, confirming the Law (which came) before me, and giving glad tidings of an Apostle to come after me, whose name shall be Ahmad.' But when he came to them with Clear Signs, they said, 'This is evident sorcery!'

Moslems claim that in the original Greek manuscript the word was spelt *paraklutos*, meaning 'a praised one', having the same meaning as 'Ahmed', but that the Christians altered the spelling to *parakletos* in order to get rid of Christ's testimony to Mohammed as His successor. What they fail to realise is that we have hundreds of ancient Greek manuscripts of the scriptures, (or portions of them), which include this verse. In not a single case is there any variation in the spelling of *parakletos*. Not one manuscript has the spelling *paraklytos* (When the Greek 'u' (upsilon) is translated into English it is not translated by the English 'u' but by 'y' (gamma) and spelt *paraklytos*).

The above evidence of the New Testament manuscripts is not the only evidence which proves that in John 14:16 Christ is referring to the Holy Spirit, and not Mohammed.

Christ said that the Holy Spirit was to be given to His disciples shortly after His ascension (Luke 24:49; Acts 1:4-6; John 7:37-39). The following verses reveal the fulfilment of the promise: Acts 2:1-4, 33, 38; 1 Corinthians 12:13; Ephesians 1:13, 14; 5:18; Romans 8:9, 11, 13-16. This came about hundreds of years before Mohammed who was not born until circa AD 570.

Let us also note the following:

a. The Spirit was to indwell believers and be the source of their power and success in witness to Christ (John 14:16; Acts 1:8).

b. He was to indwell them 'forever' (John 14:16).

c. The reason the world could not receive Him, was because they could not see Him, or know Him as He is an invisible spiritual Being (John 14:17).

d. The Holy Spirit was not to speak of Himself, unlike Mohammed. He was only to speak of Christ (John 16:13; 15:26).

e. The Holy Spirit was to help people remember all the things that Christ had spoken (John 14:26).

f. He was to convict men of sin for not believing in Christ (John 16:8, 9).

g. He was to reveal to Christ's disciples things to come (John 16:13).

h. He was to guide them into all truth so that their testimony in preaching and writing would be divine truth in everything (John 16:13).

i. His one ministry would have, for its object, the glory of Christ, not Mohammed (John 16:14).

The only unpardonable sin is blasphemy against the Holy Spirit, who is therefore a Divine Person because only God can be blasphemed (Matt. 12:31, 32). This also conclusively proves that Christ has made full payment for all other sins, since God cannot forgive sins accept on the ground of Christ's bearing for us the curse of the Law.

The Moslem who is a true seeker after God must choose between the unknowable God of the Koran and the God of the Bible. The God of the

Bible has revealed Himself through Jesus Christ as the God of Redemption, giving the gift of Eternal Life to those who accept who He is and what He has done for us. In contrast, no statements can be made positively or factually concerning Allah since he is spoken of as 'Unknowable.'

9

Moslems and the Koran

If Allah is not bound to do what is righteous then there can be no certainty as to what he may decide to do on the Judgement Day. Allah is a dictator whose decisions are inconsistent and arbitrary. One Muslim tradition relates that in a certain village two men died about the same time. One was a pious Muslim who always kept the fast, said his prayers, had gone on a pilgrimage to Mecca and observed the law of God. The other man totally neglected his religious duties and did all manner of evil. One night the village priest had a dream, in which he saw the good man writhing in the torments of hell, and the evil man enjoying the wine and houris (maidens) of paradise. When in his dream he complained to God of this obvious injustice, Allah replied: 'Have I not the right to do as I please with my own?'

Belief in such an inconsistent God must lead to great fear, as does the belief that salvation depends on good works outweighing evil works. This fear arises because no-one can be sure that he has done enough! Another Muslim tradition (Shi'a) says, 'Ali fainted seventy times a night from fear of the Day of Judgement.'

The difference between the God of the Bible and Allah of the Koran is so great. Allah has decreed both the good and bad actions of all men, whilst in the Bible all men's actions are seen as their own choice. In the Koran we see that Allah has predestined the majority of men to damnation. In the Bible we see that God has made a way for all to come to repentance. He has provided salvation for all men. In the Koran salvation depends on one's own personal merits. No-one living by his or her own merits can have the joy and peace that comes from knowing he is saved already. In the Bible every believer in Christ already possesses eternal salvation. It is gift that has been given to him and he cannot lose it (John 5:24; 10:28-29; Matt. 15:13; Rom. 8:35-39). In the Koran there can be no Father-child relationship with God, since God is only seen as the unknowable Creator. The decrees of this Creator also make prayer absolutely useless – everything has already been predetermined! In the Bible, God is 'Our Father in Heaven,' and believers are the children of God in the spiritual sense. As the anthropologist Wilhelm Schmidt has shown in his monumental work *The Origin of Religion*, even the most primitive tribes have a name for God which means 'father', as does the name 'Jupiter' which the Romans give to their supreme deity.

In the paradise of the Koran, its joys are all to be found in natural enjoyments of the 'wine and women' type. Nothing is said of enjoying fellowship with Allah. In the Bible, the believer's chief joy on earth is 'fellowship with the Father, and with His Son Jesus Christ' (1 John 1:3). In heaven, with its multiplicity of eternal joys, the supreme and surpassing joy of the redeemed will be seeing God face to face with unclouded vision. We will have unhindered fellowship with Him (Rev. 22:3, 4; 21:3).

The Allah of the Koran is the unknowable, because he has not created man in his image, or after his likeness. In light of this one can hardly call the Koran a revelation. It conceals the very God it is supposed to reveal. In the Bible we find things vastly different. The God of the Bible creates us in His likeness (Gen. 1:26). We are created moral beings with the ability to communicate with God through the medium of language. Love, justice, mercy, truth, goodness, righteousness and evil are to mean the same thing for man as they do for God. With Allah this is not so, hence the impossibility of ever knowing Him. This is illustrated by Ibn Hazm's comment on the Koran's use of the term 'merciful', which stands at the head of every Sura. He writes:

'While the Koran uses the name for God which means "the most merciful of those who show mercy", this cannot mean that he is merciful in the way that we understand the word. For God is evidently not merciful. He tortures His children with all manner of sickness, warfare, and sorrow. What then does the Koran mean? Simply that merciful is one of God's names, a name that is not in any way descriptive of God or throws any light on his nature. We use it because the Koran uses it, but do not pretend to understand what is meant by it.'

The Moslem who is a true seeker after God needs to choose between the unknowable Allah of the Koran, and the God of the Bible who has revealed Himself fully through Jesus Christ. In Jesus Christ we see that He is the God of Redemption, and is life eternal (John 17:3).

The Effects of Moslem Beliefs
S. B. John, in his book, *The Finality of Christ*, says:

The conception of God finds its reflex in the Moslem view of man. If God be conceived as Supreme Will, the highest relation that man can attain to is that of a servant. There can be nothing in the way of fellowship. Hence, quite logically, Islam is the name of this religion. It demands unhesitating and unquestioning obedience....

Upon its womankind, the blighting effect has fallen most. Arbitrariness in God creates the standard for arbitrariness in human relations, and woman, as the weaker vessel, has always been the victim of man's caprice in the Moslem world. She is not his equal, or his companion.... she exists for his pleasure, and every kind of degradation has been hers. It is significant that contact with Western culture and Christian ideas produces a revolt among Moslem woman against their position of servitude.

Dr Elder in his book, *Biblical Approach to the Muslim*, writes:

'The Koran asserts that man is superior to woman. In Sura 4:34 we read:

"Men are the protectors and maintainers of women, because God has given the one more (strength) than the other, and because they support them from their means. Therefore the righteous women are devoutly obedient, and guard in (the husband's) absence what God would have them guard. As to those women on whose part ye fear disloyalty and ill-conduct, admonish them (first), (next), refuse to share their beds, (and last) beat them (lightly); but if they return to obedience seek not against them means (of annoyance)."'

Moslem teachers, showing some compassion, have ruled that in beating his wife a man 'must use a rod no thicker than his thumb.' They have also tried to 'water down' the mention of beating by including the word 'lightly', which is not in the Arabic!

The Koran also legalises polygamy. Sura 4:3 reads:

'If ye fear that ye shall not be able to deal justly with the orphans marry women of your choice, two or three, or four; but if ye fear that ye shall not be able to deal justly (with them), then only one, or (a captive) that your right hands possess. That will be more suitable, to prevent you from doing injustice.'

Throughout the 1,300 years of Islam their scholars have said the meaning of 'equably' is that a man must treat all his wives alike in material things. If he gives a ring or dress to one, he must do the same for the others. However the Koran does not imply this, and Mohammed did not go along with the practice. He caused friction in his household because he made it evident that Ayesha was his favourite wife.

Interestingly, in modern times many Moslem teachers interpret this verse in a new way. This interpretation may have sprung from contact with nations where polygamy is a crime. Possibly they realised that women rebel against the thought of husbands having other wives. In any event these teachers are now opposing polygamy, and claim that in this verse Mohammed is actually forbidding polygamy, because it is impossible for a man to treat several wives equally as far as his feelings are concerned. Therefore they say that a man should take only one wife.

The Lord Jesus' teaching gave no preference to men over women. The laws of His kingdom were equally for both.

Devout and wealthy women followed Him from Galilee and provided for the group from their means. He welcomed Mary of Bethany as a student when she sat at His feet to learn His teaching. Although she was a foreigner and a sinner, Jesus taught the woman at Jacob's well about the water of life. Among His last words from the cross was His command to John to care for His mother. It was to a woman, Mary Magdalene, that he first revealed Himself after His resurrection (John 4:28-30, 39). Even prostitutes found Him sympathetic and understanding, as He restored them to a new dignity (John 4:13-15; 8:7-11; Matt. 21:31).

In the Church itself we find women not only placed in the same category as men (in relation to everything spiritual, Gal. 3:28), but they also received the gifts of the Holy Spirit equally with male disciples (Acts 2:17, 18; 21:9; 1 Cor. 11:4-5). Not only in the Church, but in every sphere of life, Christ's teaching and example has liberated women socially and politically, as well as indirectly through teaching children at home.

The relationship of husbands and wives is set before us in Ephesians 5:22-33, where the headship in domestic relations is vested in the husband. The husband is exhorted to love his wife 'as Christ loved the Church', with a pure sacrificial love, as he himself acknowledges the headship of Christ in his personal life. The husband's authority is Christ's authority in his own life delegated through him, and does not extend beyond or outside of Christ's authority in his own life.

10

Mohammed's Claims
for the Koran Questioned

In his book *Islam and Christian Theology*, J. W. Sweetman gives evidence that Mohammed depended on human sources for the Koran, and that its claim to be pure Arabic is not founded on fact. Amongst other information he says that:

a. The name used for the Deluge (Tufan), is a foreign word and is found in the Targum of Onkelos (Gen. 7).

b. We are told that Abraham's father was an idolator whom he wished to convert to Monotheism. This addition may be traced to the Midrash Rabba on Genesis (para. 38).

c. Like the Koranic account, the Rabbis recorded how the hand of Moses became leprous before Pharaoh, which is not Biblical.

d. The Koran claims that Pharaoh claimed divinity, this being in line with Jewish legend contained in Midrash Rabba on Exodus, para. 5.

e. The Koran also states that Pharaoh repented (10:39ff). This equates with a similar tale of Pirke Rabbi Eliezer, section 45.

f. The references to seven heavens, circles, strongholds and courses (Suras 2:29; 23:17, 86 etc.) have great affinity with the Talmud (Chagiga 96:12). Reference should also be made to the Slavomic Enoch 3:21.

g. Concerning the description of the Last Things, Yajay and Mujay (Sura 18:93-97) are the Gog and Magog of Ezekiel 38, 39.

h. The special use of 'Kaffara' in Sura 47:2, importing 'absolution', is associated with Jewish and Christian ideas of atonement.

i. Solomon was a great magician who had control of demons, spirits and winds (Sura 38:34-37). This should be compared with the account in the Second Targum of the Book of Esther, and is possibly derived from a mistaken interpretation of Ecclesiastes 2:8.

j. The account in Sura 3 opens with the story of the immaculate conception of the Virgin Mary, as found in the *Protevangelium of James*. The *Protevangelium of James* is an apocryphal book of the second century AD.

k. After this we find the Miracles of the Infancy – that Jesus spoke in His cradle, and made clay birds and breathed into them. These are parallel to the stories in the Arabic Gospel of the Infancy (32), and in the apocryphal Gospel of Thomas.

l. Ablutions before prayer are commanded in the Talmud, and in Sura 5:7 of the Koran.

m. No clear distinction is made between angels and jinn. In Sura 2:30, Satan appears as one of the angels, and as one of the jinn in Sura 18:50. A similar conclusion appears in the 'Book of Jubilee' 2:2 (Jewish pseudepigraphia where we read that the jinn were made of fire).

n. Satan is spoken of in the Koran under the name 'Shaytan', which is the equivalent, and the name 'Iblis', which is a corruption of the Greek 'Diabolos'. He is represented as the head of a host, and it is interesting to find the plurality of Satans (Shaytin) in the Koran, having a parallel in the Book of Enoch.

o. The Koran contains many references to Gabriel as the agent of revelation, and he is identified with the Holy Spirit. The Book of Jubilees 32:31 speaks of an angel bringing down seven tablets of revelation to Jacob. In a fragment of the 'Prayer of Joseph' (23:15) reserved in Pilocalia, we read: 'For I have read in the tablets of heaven all that shall befall you and your sons.' This agrees with the reference of Sura 7:145, where the heavenly tablets are said to contain details of everything.

p. Mohammed's usage of language such as 'nabi' (prophet) and 'nabuwwa' (prophecy) are borrowed from the older religions. Wright, in *Comparative Grammar* (p. 46), states that they are of Jewish-Arabic origin. Yet again this refutes Mohammed's claim that the Koran is pure Arabic.

11

Christ is the Prophet
spoken about by Moses

Muslim publications such as 'Mohammed in the Bible' state that Jesus never claimed to be the prophet spoken of by Moses. Other publications, such as 'The Bible, The Koran and Science', state that Jesus was mistaken in saying that Moses wrote of Him. We now turn to deal with these two views before looking at the doctrines of God, Christ, the Holy Spirit and Salvation.

Mohammed, (who claimed to be the prophet like Moses), never made any predictions and admitted he could not prophesy when others challenged him. His reply to the challenge was to say that the Koran was so great a miracle that it rendered prophecy on his part quite unnecessary to vindicate his claims.

Professor Abdu'l-Ahad, the author of the book *Mohammed in the Bible* clearly believes that Deuteronomy 18:18 must point to Mohammed. In the forward of his book he writes:

If these words do not apply to Mohammed they are still unfulfilled. Jesus never claimed to be the Prophet alluded to. Even His disciples were of the same opinion: they looked to a Second Coming of Jesus for the fulfilment of the prophecy (Acts 3:21). So far it is undisputed that the first coming of Jesus was not the advent of the 'Prophet like unto Moses', and His Second Coming can hardly fulfil the words. Jesus, as is believed by His Church, will appear as Judge and not as Lawgiver; but the promised one has to come with a 'fiery law' in his right hand.

From the time that Mohammed made the claim that he was this Prophet, both Jews and Christians have totally rejected his belief as sheer delusion, and proved it from the Scriptures, which the Koran claims to attest as the Word of God.

In the book of Deuteronomy we have Moses speaking to the Jewish people. God speaks through Moses and says that a prophet like Moses will arise from among their own brothers (18:15 and 18:18). It is impossible for this to refer to the Muslim nation, and Moses' meaning can be clearly understood from looking at the beginning of Deuteronomy 18 where we read:

> The priests, who are Levites – indeed the whole tribe of Levi – are to have no allotment or inheritance with Israel....They shall have no inheritance among their brothers; the LORD is their inheritance, as he promised them.

The words 'among their brothers' clearly refer to the other eleven tribes of Israel. Common sense tells us that this is also the case in Deuteronomy 18, clearly revealing that the prophecy cannot refer to Mohammed.

Mohammed is of the seed of Ishmael, who was the product of Abraham's relationship with his slave girl Hagar. Yet the promise that God made to Abraham involved his wife Sarai bearing a child, Isaac (Gen. 21:1-6), from whom Israel would arise.

Since there were many prophets who came after Moses we can assume that the one like Moses must be like him in a unique way. Although Muslims like to point out what they think are similarities between Moses and Mohammed, these similarities can be used of any prophet. But they can only truly apply to one who was uniquely like Moses. This person is Jesus, as we shall now see.

Both Jesus and Moses were raised up as mediators of covenants between God and man.

Through Moses God made the Covenant of Law with Israel at Sinai (Exod. 24:1-8), and in Jesus we have the only Mediator of the New Covenant (1 Tim. 2:5; Heb. 12:22-24; Matt. 26:26-28). Both Moses and Jesus also knew God 'face to face' and confirmed their offices with signs and wonders.

As already stated, Mohammed did not come from one of the tribes of Israel. Neither was he the Mediator of any Covenant, and certainly performed no miracles, as Sura 6:37 states.

Adding still further to the evidence already provided we see Scripture revealing that:

a. Many of the people who saw Jesus thought He was the prophet:

> 'After the people saw the miraculous sign that Jesus did, they began to say, "Surely this is the Prophet who is to come into the world' (John 6:14).

b. The disciples were aware that Moses had spoken of Jesus:

> 'We have found the one Moses wrote about in the Law, and about whom the prophets also wrote – Jesus of Nazareth' (John 1:45).

c. Jesus' words confirmed that He was the One spoken of by Moses:

> 'Do not think I will accuse you before the Father. Your accuser is Moses, on whom your hopes are set. If you believed Moses, you would believe me, for he wrote about me. But since you do not believe what he wrote, how are you going to believe what I say?' (John 5:45-47).

The disciples looked to the Second Coming of Jesus to fulfil the prophecy of Acts 3:21, yet they also clearly saw Jesus' first coming as the fulfilment of Deuteronomy 18:15, 18.

Professor Abdul-Ahad would also have us

believe that it is Mohammed who is the bringer of 'fiery law'. However, the law of Mohammed disproves its claims to be divine law by its licence towards sexual indulgence and its sanction of polygamy and concubinage. His 'law' speaks of sanctioning slavery, child marriage, easy divorce for men, the scourging of wives, as well as its doctrine of the inferiority of women to men, and its bondage of women by its customs!

12

Messianic Prophecy

Professor Dawud, another well-known Muslim scholar, does not believe that Jesus claimed to be the Messiah. Instead he believes Jesus foretold that Mohammed would be the Messiah. Yet His claim is based upon a fourteenth-century forgery called 'The Gospel of Barabbas'. This in turn is thought to have been based on a much earlier Gnostic document, of which only a fragment has been preserved.

The Gospel of Barnabus accuses Paul of altering the message of Jesus by making him to be the Incarnate Son of God and Saviour of the world. Orthodox Muslims reject the book because it contradicts the Koran (stating Jesus is not the Messiah). However they still desire to use the book to prove that Jesus was only a prophet. They also quote the book as if it was by Barnabus, the companion of Paul, to discredit Paul's doctrine of Christ!

The Koran gives the title 'Messiah' to Jesus, and pronounces judgement on the Jews for rejecting

Him as such. Seeing that the Koran applies the title 'Messiah' to Jesus should cause Muslims to stop and asked themselves the question: What did 'Messiah' mean as a title given only to Jesus of Nazareth?

Since 'Messiah' is a God-given title we need only look to Him for an explanation of the meaning. God would not give such a title to Jesus without also giving an explanation as to how this title distinguishes Jesus from others.

Professor Dawud acknowledges that there are prophecies in the Old Testament which represent Messiah as God Incarnate (God clothed in the flesh) and the Saviour of the world by His death and resurrection. Yet he states that they are false. He does not take into account the fact that the Jews were hardly likely to forge such scriptures since they did not believe them. It is also impossible for Christ's disciples to have inserted them into Jewish Scriptures, which were so closely guarded against alteration. Professor Dawud also seems to have ignored the statement made in Sura, Cattle v115, which reads:

'The Word of thy Lord doth find its fulfilment in truth and in justice: None can change His Words: For He is the one Who heareth and knoweth all.'

'Therefore the Lord himself will give you a sign: The virgin will be with child and will give birth to a son, and will call him Immanuel' (Isa. 7:14).

'For to us a child is born, to us a son is given, and the government will be on his shoulders. And he will be called Wonderful Counsellor, Mighty God, Everlasting Father, Prince of Peace (Isa. 9:6).

In scripture we find the word 'Mashiah', which means 'anointed one'. The term was applied to the High Priest (Lev. 4:23); the King (2 Sam. 1:14) and also to prophets of God (Ps. 105:15). It speaks of these men being set apart by God for God, and with the power of God helping them. However, at a later date we find Daniel predicting that after the rebuilding of Jerusalem (destroyed by Nebuchad-nezzar) a period of time would pass after which the Messiah (meaning Anointed One) would come (Dan. 9:25). In this prophecy he uses the word 'Messiah' as a title. This caused the Jews to speak freely of the one to come as 'The Messiah'. Scripture reveals that the one to come will be the supreme Anointed One. He will be the one who fulfils the offices of prophet, priest and king, which were only shadows that pointed to Him.

When Jesus stood before the Sanhedrin (the High Court of the Jews), the High Priest asked Him: 'Are you the Christ, (meaning 'Anointed One', 'Messiah') the Son of the Blessed One?' (Mark 14:61). In his reply Jesus stated that he was, and this, along with Jesus' other words, were taken as implying deity. The High Priest realised what Jesus meant in His words, and tore his own clothes, saying: 'Why do we need any more witnesses? You have heard the blasphemy. What do you think?'

In light of all we have shown it is quite clear that Jesus as the Messiah, is so much more than just a prophet.

> A shoot will come up from the stump of Jesse; from his roots a Branch will bear fruit. The Spirit of the LORD will rest on him – the Spirit of wisdom and of understanding, the Spirit of counsel and of power, the Spirit of knowledge and of the fear of the LORD – and he will delight in the fear of the LORD.... In that day the Root of Jesse will stand as a banner for the peoples; the nations will rally to him, and his place of rest will be glorious' (Isa. 11:1-3, 10).

Blessing would come to God's people through a Ruler who comes from the stump of Jesse. Although the Davidic dynasty (Jesse was David's father) would one day be like a tree stump, a Ruler would arise (hence 'a shoot'). Verse one of the above reveals the humanity of the Messiah ('a shoot from the stump of Jesse'), whilst the final part (v. 10) reveals His Deity (the 'root of Jesse'). The Messiah was not going to be One who came down from heaven in all power and glory. Instead He would come to serve (at the Second Coming He will return in all glory). Although He was before Jesse (hence root) he would limit Himself, arising as 'the shoot', speaking of the Incarnation (God clothing Himself in flesh). Why? To live a life no other could live, and then give that life as a perfect sacrifice for sin.

> 'Tell him this is what the LORD Almighty says: "Here is the man whose name is the Branch, and he will branch out from his place and build the temple of the LORD. It is he who will build the temple of the LORD, and he will be clothed with majesty and will sit and rule on his throne. And he will be a priest on his throne. And there will be harmony between the two"' (Zech. 6:12-13).

In Old Testament times a priest did not sit upon a throne. Instead he *stood* in service before the Lord. Yet in Jesus we see both the role of King and of Priest fulfilled. He is the one who came and gave His life so that others might live.

The Uniqueness of Prophecy
Biblical prophecy (including Messianic prophecy) is unique amongst all the religious books of the world. It covers a vast period of time and includes all the nations involved in the history of Israel. The prophecies reveal God as the only God of history. He is the master of all events and can work through both good and bad to bring about His purposes. One example of this perfect mastery of all events is seen in Micah's prophecy foretelling the birth of Christ in Bethlehem:

But you, Bethlehem Ephrathah, though you are small among the clans of Judah, out of you will come for me one who will be ruler over Israel, whose origins are from of old, from ancient times (Micah 5:1).

That the above prophecy refers to Christ is seen from Matthew 2:1:

After Jesus was born in Bethlehem in Judea, during the time of King Herod, Magi from the east came to Jerusalem...

During the time of the Roman Empire, several special taxations were ordered. Under the rule of Caesar Augustus one of these taxations was levied four years before the birth of Jesus. The Jewish people protested against this order, yet were overruled. However this delayed the enforcement of this taxation order for four years, bringing us to the time of Jesus' birth. Under the order Joseph and Mary were required to be present in Bethlehem (Luke 2:1-7) and so prophecy was fulfilled. Mary and Joseph later returned to Nazareth, thus fulfilling Messianic prophecy that stated the Messiah would be called a Nazarene (Matt. 2:23).

Jesus clearly reveals that Messianic prophecy points to Him:

You diligently study the Scriptures because you think that by them you possess eternal life. These are the Scriptures that testify about me, yet you refuse to come to me to have life.... If you believed Moses, you would believe me, for he wrote about me;' (John 5:39, 46. See also: Matt. 5:17, 21:42; 22:41-45; 26:24,31,56; Mark 12:10; 14:27,62; Luke 4:16-21; 18:31-33; 22:37).

Messianic prophecy is one of many infallible proofs concerning the truth of the gospel and Christ's claims within it. Messianic prophecy shows us, among other things, the kind of Person the Messiah was to be when He came. It also reveals when and where He would arrive, and how He would be born. Herman Newmark, a Hebrew Christian, in His leaflet entitled 'Prophecies of Centuries Fulfilled in a Day' lists twenty-nine prophecies occurring in twenty-four hours in the experiences of Jesus of Nazareth. They are as follows:

1. He was to be sold for thirty pieces of silver (Zech. 11:12; Matt. 26:14-15).
2. He was to be betrayed by a friend (Ps. 55:12-14; Matt. 26:47-50; John 13:18).
3. The money obtained was to be cast to the Potter (Zech. 11:13; Matt. 27:3-10).
4. His disciples were to forsake Him (Zech. 13:7; Matt. 26:56; Mark 14:27).
5. He was to be accused by false witnesses (Ps. 55:11, 109:2; Matt. 26:59, 60).
6. He would be struck on the cheek with a rod (Micah 5:1; Matt. 26:67).

7. He was to be beaten and spat upon (Isa. 50:6; Luke 22:64).
8. His appearance was to be disfigured (Isa. 52:14; Matt. 27:29, 30
9. He was to be silent before His accusers (Isa. 53:7; Matt. 27:12-14; 1 Pet. 1:23).
10. He was to be wounded and bruised (Isa. 53:6; Matt. 27:26, 29).
11. His hands and feet were to be pierced (Ps. 22:16; Luke 23:33; John 20: 25-27).
12. He was to be crucified with the wicked (Isa. 53:12; Mark 15:27, 28).
13. The people were to ridicule Him (Ps. 22:8; Matt. 27:41, 43).
14. The people were to be astonished (Ps. 22:17; Isa. 52:14; Luke 23:35).
15. He was to pray for His persecutors (Isa. 53:12; Ps. 109:4; Luke 23:34).
16. The people were to shake their heads (Ps. 109:25; Matt. 27:39).
17. His garments were parted/lots cast for clothing (Ps. 22:19; John 19:24).
18. He was to cry: 'My God, My God…' (Ps. 22:1; Matt. 27:46).
19. He was to thirst (Ps. 69:3, 21; John 19:28).
20. They were to give Him gall and vinegar (Ps. 69:21; Matt. 27:34; John 19:28).
21. He was to commit Himself to God (Ps. 31:5; Luke 23:46).
22. His friends stood at a distance (Ps. 38:11; Luke 23:49).

23. His bones were not to be broken, yet were out of joint (Ps. 34:20; Exod. 12:46; Ps. 22:14, 17; John 19:31-36).
24. His side was to be pierced (Zech 12:10; John 19:34-37).
25. His heart was to be broken (Ps. 22:14; John 19:34).
26. Darkness was to cover the land (Amos 8:9; Matt. 27:45).
27. He was to be buried in a rich man's tomb (Isa. 53:9; John 10:11, 17, 18; Gal. 2:20).
28. His death was to be voluntary (Isa. 53:12; Ps. 40:6-8; John 10:11, 17).
29. His death was to be substitutionary (Isa. 53:4-6, 12; Dan. 9:26; Matt. 20:18; 1 Cor. 15:3; 1 Pet. 2:24; Rev. 1:5, 6).

These events were all fulfilled in detail in 24 hours in the experience of Jesus of Nazareth. According to the law of compound probabilities, the chance that they all happened together by accident is 1 in 537,000,000.

Neander, in his *History of Christian Dogma*, writes:

Among the strictly new truths which Christianity presents, is the doctrine of a Man in whom may be recognised the perfect union of the Divine and human. In the existing tendencies of the age there was nothing analogous, and it stands in opposition to the Jewish standpoint which places a chasm between God and man, as well as to the heathen deification of nature and man, or its depriving humanity of its characteristic qualities…. The heathen myths of transient appearances of the gods in human form, especially the incarnation of the oriental gods, are connected with Pantheism, which in all forms of existence beholds the Divine made an object of the senses, and, therefore, admits an incarnation of it in lower forms of nature. This was something altogether different from the full revelation of the Divine Essence in the form of a definite human life…. The humiliation of Christ and His death on the Cross were at variance with the conceptions of the heathen, who delighted in sensuous splendour, and adorned it with the fabled appearances of their deities. This contrariety may be known from the fabulous description of the heroes whom they set up in opposition to the power of Christianity, as in the Life of Apollonious of Tyana, by Philostratus.

During the last hundred years or so many Jewish people have been brought to believe in Jesus as their Messiah as the result of studying Messianic prophecy. The following is just one example:

Mordecai S. Bergmann was brought up in the strictest of Jewish religious sects, the Chassidim. When he was fourteen, he was sent to Breslau to study under the Chief Rabbi there. Returning later to Kalisch, he applied himself diligently to the study of the Talmud. Later in life, he came to live in London, where he organised a small synagogue, and in which he ministered for two years. Taken ill, he entered a German hospital where he remained for six weeks. While there he started to read a German Bible which was on a shelf in the ward. As a reader in the synagogue he knew the Pentateuch and portions of the prophecies by heart.

The verses in Daniel chapter 9, which record in the first portion of it Daniel's great prayer, were very familiar to him, for these verses are repeated every Monday and Tuesday by religious Jews: but the later part of the chapter which records the prophecy of the seventy weeks (of years) is never read; in fact, the rabbis pronounce a dreadful curse on anyone who investigates this prophecy. They say, 'Their bones shall rot who compute the end of time.'

Remembering this anathema, it was with fear and trembling that he went on to read the prophecy. Coming to verse 26, and reading the words, 'Messiah shall be cut off, but not for Himself,' he threw the Bible down, thinking it was a Christian Bible and altered from the Hebrew original to favour their view that Jesus of Nazareth was the Jewish Messiah. But though he did so, he could not put the words out of his mind. They sank deeper and deeper into his soul, and wherever he looked he seemed to see them in flaming Hebrew characters. The result was he was greatly disturbed in mind and heart.

After a time he again took up the Bible, and without thinking of any particular passage opened it at Isaiah chapter fifty-three. He was arrested by the words: 'For he was cut off out of the land of the living; for the transgressions of My people was he stricken' (v. 8). This seemed to be the answer to the question he had been asking himself ever since he had read the words, 'Messiah shall be cut off, but not for Himself,' and which seemed to be confronting him everywhere. For whom then, if not for Himself, was the Messiah to be cut off? Here the answer was plainly revealed to him: 'For the transgressions of my people was He stricken.'

On leaving hospital he went home, put on his phylacteries and tallith, in order to perform the prescribed prayers; but found he could not utter a single sentence of the prayer book. One message, found in Psalm 119:18, came to his mind, 'Open my eyes that I may see wonderful things in your law.' He kept on repeating it for nearly two hours. Then he left the house and walked along the street, still praying the same prayer.

The Lord led him to the home of Dr Ewald, a Jewish believer in the Lord Jesus Christ. To him he unburdened his heart. Here, for the first time, he learned that the Messiah, who was to be cut for the transgression of His people, was the Lord Jesus whom the Christian Gospels proclaimed to be the incarnate Son of God, and only Saviour of sinners, and whom the Jewish nation had rejected. After studying the Messianic prophecies diligently with the help of his friend, he accepted the Lord Jesus as his Messiah and personal Saviour.

As a result, he suffered much persecution at the hands of his former Jewish friends, but was uncompromisingly steadfast in his new faith, and was greatly blessed and used to win other Jews for Christ.

13

The Claims of Christ

In the Sermon on the Mount we read of Christ saying, 'Do not think that I have come to abolish the Law or the Prophets; I have not come to abolish them but to fulfil them' (Matt. 5:17).

This claim of Christ embraces every other claim of His made in relation to His Person and His Work. His claim to fulfil the Law and the Prophets is a claim to Deity. The prophets foretold of His Deity, and their words were 'fleshed out' in His Person. The Law demands perfect obedience to its commandments as the condition of Justification and Eternal Life, therefore Jesus' claim is to be the perfect representative of man. He also fulfilled the words of the Prophets, who spoke of His Deity. Their words were 'fleshed out' in His Person.

We also find the following claims made by Jesus:

1. Jesus claimed to have the power to forgive sins, which the Jews rightly recognised is only

possible to God, since sin is the transgression of His Law and rebellion against him (Mark 2:5-7).

2. Jesus claimed to be the Judge and lawgiver of mankind (Matt. 5:21-28; 7:21-28; 13:30-32; 21:44; 25:1-46; John 5:22, 27; 12:48).

3. Jesus said that the angels are His angels (Matt. 13:41; 16:27).

4. Jesus said that He would send prophets and wise men to His people whom they would persecute, when the true prophet is a messenger of God and sent only by Him (Matt. 23:34).

5. Jesus said that those who suffer for His sake are blessed, which is the same as suffering for righteousness sake; since God is the only one who blesses, therefore suffering persecution for His sake can make it blessed because God claims the supreme place in every life (Matt. 5:10-12).

6. Jesus claimed that at His Second Coming He will come 'in the glory of the Father' (Matt. 16:2). In the Old Testament God declares that He will not give His glory to another (Isa. 42:8). Christ claims to share in the glory incommunicable to any creature (Matt. 16:27).

7. Jesus said that those who had seen Him had seen the Father (John 14:7-9; 12:45; 15:24). Only as one in substance and attributes with the Father could Christ make this claim, for it can never be true that one who has seen only a creature has seen the Creator.

8. Jesus said that He was greater than the Temple dedicated to the worship of Jehovah (Matt. 12:6).

9. Jesus said that His knowledge of the Father was coequal with the Father's knowledge of Him – infinite (Matt. 11:27; John 10:15).

10. Jesus claimed to be Lord of the Sabbath, which God ordained for our benefit, both physical and spiritual (Gen. 2:3; Matt. 12:8).

11. Jesus stated that the will of the Father, in appointing Him to be the Judge of all men, is 'that all may honour the Son just as they honour the Father', with equal honour (John 5:22, 23).

12. Jesus' great 'I am' claims involved His Deity. He clearly identifies Himself as God, who revealed Himself to Israel as 'I Am' (Exod. 3:14). The Jews clearly understood what He was saying, and attempted to stone Him (John 8:58).

    a. 'I am the bread of life' (John 6:35, 41, 48, 51) is a claim by Christ to be in a spiritual sense all that natural food is to them physically. He is the sole means of supply for their spiritual needs, which only God could be, God also being the only one who can truly supply physical needs as well.

    b. 'I am the light of the world' (John 8:12; 9:5; 12:35, 36, 46) is a claim to be to men spiritually all that the sun is to them naturally, which of course, only God can be.

c. 'Before Abraham was, "I AM"' (John 8:58) – not 'Before Abraham was, I was,' but 'I am' – as in the eternally existing one.

d. 'I am the resurrection and the life' (John 11:25). In John 5:28, 29 and 6:38-40, Christ claimed that it will be He who will raise all the dead to life. Only omnipotence can do this.

e. 'I am the door' (John 10:9) is a claim to be the only Saviour of sinners, that He is the only way of access into the fold of salvation. As has already been stated in previous pages, only a Saviour who is Deity incarnate could both save us from the wrath of God and provide for us justifying righteousness and eternal life.

f. 'I am the way and the truth and the life. No man comes to the Father but by Me' (John 14:6). Jesus is the way of approach to God, and the truth concerning God revealed to man. He is the giver of the eternal life that fits man for fellowship with God as holy (John 3:14-16; 5:40; 6:33-35, 40, 47-51, 53-58; 10:10).

g. Jesus claimed for Himself the name 'I AM,' by which God revealed Himself through Moses to Israel, when the soldiers came to arrest him (John 18:3-6). 'Jesus knowing all that was going to happen to him, went out and asked them, "Who is it you want?" "Jesus of Nazareth," they replied. "I am" ('he' is not in the original), Jesus said. (And Judas the traitor was standing there with them.) When Jesus said, "I am," they drew back and fell to the ground.'

The Jewish Charges of Blasphemy

The Jewish charges of blasphemy against Jesus completely disprove the view of all who deny that Christ claimed to be God incarnate. For example, in Mark 2:7 we read of the Jews charging Christ with blasphemy. This was because He claimed the power to forgive sins. They rightly recognised that only God can forgive sins, since sin is a transgression of His Law. Christ accepted their interpretation of His claims to forgive sins as a claim to Deity. If their interpretation had been wrong His honesty and common sense would have brought forth an instant denial to such a claim, along with the correct interpretation to His words. However, instead of a denial we find Him going on to perform a miracle of divine healing to prove His right to make such a claim. This was a miracle that only the power of God could have brought about (Mark 2:8-11).

In John 5:18 we read, 'For this reason the Jews tried all the harder to kill him, not only was he breaking the Sabbath, but he was even calling God his own Father, making himself equal with God.'

The Jews themselves claimed that God was their Father (John 8:41), on the basis of such passages as Exodus 4:22 and Isaiah 1:2. Yet their desire to kill Jesus 'for calling God his own Father' shows that they understood Jesus to be claiming a totally different kind of sonship (hence John 3:16: For God so loved the world that He sent his ONLY Son). His claim was to divine sonship. Thus it was a claim to being equal with God.

In John 8:56-59 there is another instance of the Jews accusing Christ of claiming Deity after He said, 'Before Abraham was, I AM,' this being the name by which God made Himself known to the people of Israel (Exod. 3:13-14). On saying, 'Before Abraham was, I AM,' the Jews took up stones to stone Jesus. Once again He accepted their interpretation of His claim as a claim to Deity.

Liddon, in his *The Divinity of Our Lord*, writes; 'Our Lord says not: "Before Abraham was, I was," but "I AM." He claims pre-existence indeed, but He does not merely claim pre-existence. He unveils a consciousness of Eternal Being. He speaks as if one to whom time has no effect, for whom it has no meaning. He is the "I AM" of ancient Israel. He knows no past, as He knows no future; He is the unbeginning, unending Being; He is the Eternal "NOW." This is the plain sense of His language.'

In John 10:31 we again read of the Jews taking up stones to stone Christ for blasphemy. He had said 'I and the Father are One,' which they recognised as a claim to oneness in power, and therefore to Deity. On this occasion Jesus replies to their accusation in an interesting way. He says: 'Is it not written in your Law, "I have said you are gods"? If he called them "gods", to whom the word of God came – and the Scripture cannot be broken – what about the one whom the Father set apart as his very own and sent into the world?'

In Judaism the idea of the complete separation of God from man prevented all ideas of divine incarnation in man. Therefore, instead of quoting any of the many passages which revealed that Messiah would be Deity Incarnate, Jesus quoted Psalm 82:6 as a bridge to help His hearers cross over to the idea of Divine Incarnation in the Messiah.

Godet writes:

The monotheism of the Bible is absolutely different to that cold, dead Deism extracted by Jewish orthodoxy from the sacred writings, and separating man by a great gulf from his Creator.... Every theocratic function conferred by, and exercised in the name of God, places him (to whom it is entrusted), in a living relation with the Most High, making him share His inspiration, and constitutes him His agent. Thereby the man, whether king, judge, or prophet, becomes relatively a manifestation of God Himself: 'In that day, the house of David shall be as God, as the angel of the Lord' (Zech. 12:8). The Old Testament is, in its deepest tendency, ever advancing towards the incarnation, the climax of the increasing approximation between God and man. It is on this that our Lord's argument is really based: if there be nothing blasphemous in the whole current, the end to which it is flowing – the appearance of a man who declares Himself one with God has nothing in itself derogatory to the sovereignty of God.

Neander says on this point: 'Christ sought to prove to their apprehension that the idea of a communication of the Divine Majesty to human nature was by no means foreign to the revelations of the Old Testament. If the gulf between God and all things finite were impassable, it must have been blasphemy in any sense to attribute the name Elohim to mortal men.'

Looking back to John 10:31ff we see that the Jews recognised that Christ's words were not a disclaimer to Deity. They still sought to stone Him because of the prejudice already built up in their minds. His words did not fit into their framework of thinking, and so they assumed that He must be wrong, not thinking that they themselves might be in error.

In John 19:7, we read of the Jewish leaders saying to Pilate, 'We have a law and according to that law he must die, because he claimed to be the Son of God.'

In Luke 18:19 we find a certain ruler asking Jesus, 'Good teacher, what must I do to inherit eternal life?' Jesus' reply is very interesting. He

says, 'Why do you call me good? No one is good
– except God alone.'

Many of those around Jesus did not accept His
claims to Deity. Yet the ruler saw Jesus as good.
Christ's reply is given to make the man think. Jesus
is saying, 'You call me good – but none is good
except God. Why are you calling me good?' In
these words He seeks to help the ruler understand
the truth. Only God is good, and the ruler sees
Jesus as good, therefore Jesus must be much more
than just a teacher.

There are those who would have us believe
that Jesus never claimed to be God. However,
in looking at the Scriptures, we have seen that
unbelievers clearly understood Jesus' claims to
Deity, and sought to have Him put to death
because of those very claims.

We also note the following:

1. Scripture clearly reveals that Christ accepted
   worship, which is the exclusive prerogative of
   God (Matt. 8:22; 9:18; 14:33; 15:25; 28:9,17;
   Mark 5:6; 15:19; Luke 24:52; John 9:38).
   The apostles and the angel who showed John
   the visions he describes in the Book of the
   Revelation, refused the worship which Jesus
   accepted (Acts 10:25; 14:8-15; Rev. 19:10;
   22:8-9).
2. Christ claimed to be able to give rest to all
   the weary and heavy-laden who come to Him
   (Matt. 11:28).

3. Christ claimed to exercise the power of control over the forces of nature (Matt. 8:26; Mark 4:35-41; Luke 8:22-25).

4. Christ claimed that all that the Father has are His also (John 17:10). No created being could say this.

5. Christ claimed to exercise control over the world of evil spirits. They acknowledged His authority over them, and that He is to be their Judge on the Judgement Day (Mark 5:1-13; Matt. 8:29-33).

6. Christ claimed that all things which the Father did, He did also (John 5:19).

7. Christ claimed omniscience in claiming to know how the people of Tyre, Sidon and Sodom would have reacted to His miracles had they only witnessed them – by the repentance of a lasting faith (Matt. 11:20-24). Christ also claimed and manifested His omniscience in the matter of the tribute money (Matt. 17:24-27).

8. In Revelation 1:8 Christ calls Himself 'the Almighty' – a title Arians admit can apply only to Jehovah. Arians seek to avoid the claims of Christ to Deity in saying that the verse applies to the Father. But since it is Christ who is referred to in the previous verse it is common sense to apply the title to Christ as emphasising that the One who is to come in the clouds at His Second Coming (Dan. 7:13; Matt. 24:30; Mark 14:62) is the Almighty,

Deity Incarnate. Several Messianic prophecies relating to His Second Coming give Him the title 'Jehovah' (Isa. 40:9,10; Zech. 2:8-11; 14:1-5; Isa. 12:6; 24:23; Zeph. 3:14-17; Joel 3:16, 17; Micah 4:6, 7; 5:1). Apart from this the One who claims to be the 'Almighty' claims, in the same verse, to be the 'Alpha and Omega,' and without dispute Christ calls Himself by the title in Revelation 22:12-13.

9. Christ applied to Himself titles given to Jehovah in the Old Testament. The title 'bridegroom' is given to Jehovah in Hosea 2:19, 20; Isaiah 54:5 and Jeremiah 3:14. Christ calls Himself by this title in Mark 2:20; Matthew 22:1-14 and 25:1-13. Paul gives this title to Christ in 2 Corinthians 11:2 and Ephesians 5:23-32. The apostle John uses it of Christ in Revelation 19:7; 21:9; 22:17, as did John the Baptist in speaking of his relationship to Christ (John 3:29).

10. 'Shepherd' is another title given to Jehovah in the Old Testament and to Messiah. It is given to Jehovah in Genesis 49:24; Psalms 23:1; 80:1; Jeremiah 31:10 and Ezekel 34:6-31. In Isaiah 40:9-11 it is given to the Messiah as the God-man, for the reference is to His Second Coming. In Zecheriah 2:8-11; 12:7-10; 14:1-5, Messiah is called both 'Jehovah of hosts' (Zech 2:8), and also 'Jehovah' (2:10, 11; 9:14-17; 14:1-5; Isa. 35:4; 63:1-6; Zeph. 3:8-20; Joel 3:9-21). Jesus is the good Shepherd John 10:1-21.

Christ's Promise of the Holy Spirit

In John 15:26 Jesus tells His disciples that He, along with the Father, will send them the Holy Spirit. As we shall see below, Scripture clearly reveals that the Holy Spirit is a Divine Person – and not a Divine influence. Therefore in His promise to the disciples we see another indication of the Deity of Christ. This is because no created being, however great, could send a Divine Person to indwell man.

Evidence for the Person of the Holy Spirit is clearly seen in the following:

1. The assertion 'God is Spirit' (John 4:24) cannot refer to an impersonal influence, since it would make God no more than an influence. It is man's possession of spirit as distinct from soul – which he shares with animals – which makes him a person, because he possesses a moral nature. It is 'spirit' that gives man the capacity for God-consciousness, and therefore 'spirit' alone is personal. Since it is spirit in man alone that makes him personal, it is impossible that the Spirit of God should be impersonal, else the effect would be greater than the cause.

2. An influence does not possess a mind, yet Romans 8:27 tells us that God knows the mind of the Spirit.

3. An influence does not possess feelings or emotions; nor can it pray. Yet the Holy Spirit 'intercedes for us with groans that words cannot express'.

4. An influence, when good, only brings honour to the person from whom it proceeds. Yet the Spirit, proceeds from the Father, and has, for the object of His ministry, the glory of Christ (John 16:14).

5. An influence cannot be blasphemed, yet Jesus said that the only sin that cannot be forgiven is blasphemy against the Holy Spirit (Matt. 12:31-32). The fact that all other sins can be forgiven shows that Jesus has paid the price for them all. If people reject the word of the Holy Spirit, who informs us of what Christ has done, they can never be forgiven. They are effectively saying 'God is a liar – His way is not right.'

6. When Ananias and Sapphira lied to the Holy Spirit (Acts 5:3-4) they were lying to a person, since no one can lie to an influence.

7. An influence cannot be grieved, whilst the Holy Spirit can (Isa. 63:10; Eph. 4:30).

8. An influence can only bear witness to the person from whom it proceeds, it showing the kind of person he or she is. Unlike this, the Holy Spirit is sent by the Father to bear witness to Christ (John 15:26).

9. In speaking of the coming of the Holy Spirit, Christ says, 'And I will ask the Father, and he will give you another Counsellor to be with you forever.' In doing this Christ was comparing the Holy Spirit to Himself, and to His ministry, which was personal. The Greek

word for Counsellor is *parakletos* and speaks of a person called to assist another person – one who pleads the cause of another. This quality can never belong to an influence or force.

10. An influence cannot be spoken of as 'hearing'. The Holy Spirit cannot be an influence because Jesus said that the Holy Spirit spoke what He heard (John 16:13).

11. An influence cannot unveil the future, but Christ said that the Holy Spirit would declare to His disciples the things that were to come (John 16:13).

12. An influence has no capacity to decide the best course of action to be taken in given circumstances. Yet Scripture says: 'It seemed good to the Holy Spirit and to us.' (Acts 15:28).

13. An influence cannot be personified as receiving. Yet the Holy Spirit receives from Christ what He then communicates to the disciples (John 16:14, 16).

14. An influence cannot assume physical form, or materialise itself. But we know from the phenomena of Spiritism that evil spirits, impersonating the dead and Satan, can materialise themselves. So John the Baptist saw the Holy Spirit at Christ's baptism descending upon Him in the form of a dove (John 1:32-35; Matt. 3:16).

Figurative expressions are used of the Holy Spirit, yet this does not mean that He cannot be a person, since figurative expressions are also used of Christ (e.g. 'I am the Door', John 10:9).

In giving the great commission to His disciples to preach the gospel to every creature (Matt. 28:19; Mark 16:15), Christ placed His own name before that of the Holy Spirit, who is a divine person. Had Christ been only a created being, even though the greatest of them all, He could not have placed his name before that of the Holy Spirit as He does in these passages. Moreover, the singular 'name' in which believers are to be baptised – not 'names' – reveals that the Father, Son and Holy Spirit together constitute the one Being of God, even as spirit, soul, and body together speak of the one being of man.

14

Looking at the Meaning of 'Trinity'

Imagine that you arrive at the scene of an accident, and find a smashed car at the bottom of the cliff on which you are standing. The car is green, and with very large wheels and tyres – the sort you'd only find on customised cars. At the cliff edge you see the green paint on many of the rocks, and the large distinctive tyre tracks leading over the edge of the cliff. The soil was disturbed, and rocks had fallen away. Directly below were the remains of the vehicle. Logically speaking the car had slipped over the cliff. Although you were not present, and do not necessarily understand how it had happened, all the evidence (secondary factors) points to one logical conclusion: the car went over the cliff.

In this chapter we look at the Trinity. The term Trinity is not found in Scripture, but speaks of a truth seen throughout the Bible – that there are three Persons co-existing in unity as one God. As with the illustration above, we shall look at secondary factors, which point us to a logical conclusion – that God is a plurality of Persons in perfect unity as One. To attempt to understand everything about God is not possible, He being the supreme Creator. Yet to avoid issues just because they seem difficult is just as foolish.

In Genesis 1:1 we read of God in the plural, yet who creates in the singular – creating as one. Throughout the Old Testament 'Elohim' occurs 2,312 times and the alternation of singulars and plurals of the divine names effectively safeguards against interpreting Elohim as signifying a plurality of gods, and yet at the same time also safeguards against the denial of a plurality of persons within the Godhead.

Later in Deuteronomy 6:4 we read: 'Hear, O Israel: The LORD our God, the LORD is one' (Shema Yisroel Adonai Elohenu Adonai Echad). The word that is used for 'one' in this passage is not 'yachid' speaking of absolute one-ness, but 'echad' speaking of a composite one – like one football team and so forth.

In the New Testament we read of Jesus saying, 'I and the Father are one' (John 10:30), which led the Jews to want to kill Him, they recognising what He was saying – that He is God. In Greek, the word 'one' is neuter (hen), not masculine (heis), which indicates that Jesus and God were one and the same in essence and power.

Shortly after the birth of Christianity we find people speaking of the word 'Person' and saying that in the one God there are three persona, equal yet unique, being together the One True God. This may seem impossible to us, but as we look at the meaning of 'Person' things get a little clearer.

If you or I were locked in a prison cell it is obvious that we would not be able to escape – after all we cannot walk through walls. Yet, even though we are trapped bodily, our minds remain free. We could think of events that occurred in the past, create a future in our imagination, or even 'travel' around the world, so to speak, in our thoughts and so on. The mental abilities within man are vast and wonderful – each of us has millions of thoughts and millions of stories and millions of experiences. All of these are within us and so the term Person was used to speak of the place where I reside, the place where all that is 'me' is contained. Where 'me' resides there is self-consciousness, with the capability of free thought and action – this was termed full personality.

Personality cannot be measured in space or time, it can only be perceived in action, in relation with either the environment or other beings. Personality is clearly seen in the actions of the will, this being our capacity to make choices, commitments and decisions. Will is the outworking of who we are, our thoughts and beliefs. It is an expression of the choice made according to how we perceive others and 'see' life.

In this day and age our whole being – mentally, physically and spiritually – is spoken of as being a Person. But this was not the original meaning of person. The original meaning of person did not contain the physical element, which confuses us today when we think of three persons, yet one God. Three physical beings seen as persona are obviously not one God, yet when we realise that 'person' does not contain the physical element, then things get a little clearer. God expressly prohibited man from making images of Him because the image then became 'God' for us. In other words our thoughts 'made' Him, instead of letting Him speak for Himself. For example, one of the simple reasons why many in the Jewish nation rejected Jesus is because He did not fit the image they had made concerning the Messiah. Pictures of a three-headed God, or three men as being one God, do not depict the Trinity, since they fail to do justice to God's revelation of Himself.

The Latin word 'persona' was originally derived from a mask through which an actor spoke, the word person actually being two words: 'per' meaning 'through' and 'sono' meaning 'to sound.' The mask gave an indication as to where the actor behind the mask was and what he was like, and of the one he was meant to depict. For example a red mask could have been used to speak of an angry man and a black mask to speak of a murderer and death, and so forth. The mask was a 'personification' of the unseen person within, so to speak. The word soon came to be applied to the character of the actor, rather than the mask, and eventually came to mean the inner being –

the thinking, rational, self-conscious being – the place where the sum total of a man's thinking and being was to be found. Our physical frames are often thought as being the 'person' in the sense that a mask was originally described as 'person,' yet this fails to show how the idea developed, and apart from this you do not need to have a physical body to reveal personality. For example a phone call or family videotape can directly communicate personality – the body does not have to be physically present. Hence 'person' speaks of that which does not belong to the realm of space or the region of the visible, as we have already said, instead speaking more of a spirituality in time. It is the true substance of being, in space and time, yet with a final destiny beyond what we now know.

As already stated, thinking of three Persons yet one God is difficult for us since, when we look at a person, we see the whole person – body included, and seeing a material being causes us to arrive at $1+1+1=3$ when thinking of Trinity. Yet looking at things another way helps us see things in a different perspective, after all, $1 \times 1 \times 1 = 1$

We would not use a fishing-net to catch sunlight, and in looking at persona we should remember that we are not dealing with something that can be visibly seen in itself or, for example, held with our hands. This is why illustrations such as ice, water and steam being used to reveal 'three-as–oneness' convey but a very weak picture of the reality. A slightly better attempt, though still clumsy, would be to say that air is made up of oxygen, hydrogen and nitrogen.

God is a Person. He is a being whom we can encounter because He has chosen to reveal Himself to us in ways whereby we can understand who He is and what He is like. He is a perfect being and so much more than an object to be observed and so much more than our best and most 'perfect' thoughts.

We begin to realise that God is 'out there somewhere' by looking at the design in creation, yet we can only truly know Him because He has chosen to communicate with us, using the mediums of language and action to convey what He is like.

God is personal and for us; yet, due to sin, we are far from Him. However, God is a loving God who reaches out to us. Because of His grace, mercy and compassion, we are able to encounter Him through His actions and words in such a way that we 'see' and know the One who cannot otherwise be known. For instance, He presents us with pictures of Himself in the analogy of the human form. Just one example of this would be when God speaks of His arm reaching out to sustain man:

> My righteousness draws near speedily, my salvation is on the way, and my arm will bring justice to the nations. The islands will look to me and wait in hope for my arm (Isa. 51:5).

We often think that such phrases as 'my arm' are given to show that God is like us, yet this is not so. Firstly, Scripture informs us that God is Spirit (John 4:24), and secondly, God uses human terminology to reveal what He is like, and in doing so shows that He is very different from us. For example, unlike humanity, who often takes up weapons against others in indiscriminate and irrational ways, God's arm brings about His perfect justice. The one who has every right to destroy rebellious man 'reaches forth His arm to help man' instead. God always accomplishes what He sets out to do. He is far superior to us in every way, and comparison is not really possible. And yet He graciously uses anthropomorphic language so that we might see and understand who He is. God is a living being, much more than a function or conglomerate of worldly ideas reaching upwards. He is the Holy One, who stoops low in love, compassion and mercy, reaching out to those who deserve nothing, and in giving Himself, giving everything.

In today's society we often see a person as a physical being who sees his fellow man as a potential competitor in life. Or he may see others as 'stepping stones' – no more than tools to be used and abused as one marches relentlessly on to some form of worldly success. One of our problems is that we don't look at much below the surface and therefore see 'person' as little more than an isolated individual who is complete in him/herself. In the light of all this, our rationalistic thinking often sees the idea of three persons in the one God as totally impossible. Yet to be a true person speaks of having perfect out-going relationships with those around us. God did not create us to compete with one another, compare ourselves with one another, or use and abuse one-another. We were created to inter-relate in deep and wonderful ways, whilst still retaining our individuality. The word 'person' does not speak of that which is visible in itself or measurable, but of that which is present nonetheless and is revealed in its relation to others.

The 'person' of the eternal Son of God, for example, whilst having His own identity, existed in inseparable union with the 'persons' of the Father and the Holy Spirit.

Speaking of God we find three 'persons' unique yet the same, giving out and receiving love, wrapped in absolute holiness. And so we begin to catch a glimpse of three in oneness. Let's remind ourselves of this again: God is absolute perfection. He does not need to lean upon or rely upon anything to make Him who He is. He is the great 'I AM' and within the persons of the Trinity we find the binding essence of love – not a fleeting feeling, but an active willing love, which gives out and receives. There is one God and that God Triune: One God in three Persons. None of them can possibly be 'the whole God', and none of them can be God except in union with the other two Persons. The Father, Son and Holy Spirit are one, and only one God, and each has a peculiarity incommunicable to the others. None of them is God without the other two, each of them with others is God.

Today we have people who are called schizophrenic because they display more than one personality. This has come about through the fall away from God, along with unknown additional factors, and yet, in a strange way, this can help us as we look at 'person.' Within the one God we have three persons, perfectly loving, perfectly communicating, distinct, yet also the same – a powerful dynamic relationship characterised in love and holiness. The Father is the giver of unoriginated divine love, a pure source; the thinking, active, giving love of a transcendent father. The Incarnate Son is the receiver and communicator of this love – the Word made flesh. He receives glory and power from the Father and empties Himself of it, whilst being continually filled, in giving out to others. He is the perfect Mediator – pure mediation, a thinking active person, and not just an object which something passes through. The Spirit is life given and life returning to God. He is a thinking active person, not a supply of power, but a giver of Himself pointing to the work of the Son and the love of Father and Son.

Therefore in the one God we see, through perfect relationship and intimacy (which is not at the expense of unity), three Persons – Father, Son and Spirit, each characterised by their selflessness and yet so much more.

> Therefore go and make disciples of all nations, baptising them in the name of the Father and of the Son and of the Holy Spirit (Matt. 28:19).

In the above verse the word 'name' is singular. In using this word Jesus indicates that there is one God, but three distinct Persons within the Godhead – the Father, the Son, and the Holy Spirit.

15

The Word of God, and Witness of the Apostles to Christ

'In the beginning was the Word and the Word was with God and the Word was God. He was with God in the beginning' (John 1:1-2).

In the beginning God created the heavens and the earth, and made human beings with the ability to communicate with one another through language. Language is the bearer of meaning, since words help our minds to grasp what others are driving at. For example, if someone said, 'Watch out, a car is coming up behind you,' we would make sure that we moved out of its way if necessary. Communication is possible through language because all minds have at least some thoughts in common.

Scripture reveals that God communicates with us through the medium of language, helping us to see what He is like. He speaks in word and action throughout history and through His revelation we begin to realise that life, in the best meaning of the word, is only truly found in Him. God's dealings with man, throughout history, along with His promises for the future, show us that He is more than willing to break into man's dark closet of autonomy, so to speak, and 'switch on the light,' helping us to reach out to Him. Helen Keller, born blind and deaf, helps us capture something of the creative power, and enlightenment, that language brings. She writes of the effect that language had upon her mind in this way:

> Someone was drawing water and my teacher placed my hand under the spout. As the cool stream gushed over my hand she spelled into the other the word 'water', first slowly, then rapidly. I stood still, my whole attention fixed upon the motion of her fingers. Suddenly I felt a misty consciousness as of something forgotten – a thrill of returning thought; and somehow the mystery of language was revealed to me. I knew then that w-a-t-e-r meant the wonderful cool something that was flowing over my hand. The living word awakened my soul, gave it light, hope, joy, and set it free. There were barriers still, it is true, but barriers that in time could be swept away. I left the well-house eager to learn. Everything had a name and each name gave birth to a new thought. As we returned to the house, every object which I touched seemed to quiver with life, that was because I saw everything with the strange new sight that had come to me (Quoted

by A. Custance in *Who Taught Adam to Speak?* pp. 9-10).

John begins his gospels with: 'In the beginning was the Word, and the Word was with God and the Word was God.' One of the reasons he does this is because in Jesus we see, in a unique way, what God is like. A word is an expression of a hidden thought, and if we do not verbalise thinking, then others will not be able to understand us. In Greek, the Word (Logos) speaks of both things in the mind, and the words by which they are expressed. It is, therefore, the outward form by which a thing is expressed, and yet also the inward thought itself. In Jesus we see one who clearly reveals the thinking of God. Yet Jesus is not merely the abstract product of thought as the use of the pronouns in John chapter one clearly reveal.

There are those who believe that John was greatly influenced by the Greek idea contained in 'Word', and, in the light of this, would see Jesus as no more than a lesser form of God, indeed, another god, or just a prophet. Three points can be made in reply to this: firstly this claim does not take into account the fact that John is Jewish and (as are all Christians) a monotheist (believing in one God). He would hardly begin his Gospel stating that there were two gods, with the second being inferior to the first! Neither would he be over-influenced in the first few verses of his writing, only to go back to a very Jewish approach afterwards; it would be inconsistent with his thinking.

Secondly, the Greek text does not warrant the use of the indefinite article 'a' before 'God'. The purpose of the Greek grammar is to emphasise the divine nature of the Word.

> 'The omission of the indefinite article is common with nouns in the predicative construction' (F. F. Bruce, *Answers to Questions,* p. 66).

Thirdly, as we shall now see, John is drawing upon his Jewish roots much more than anything else in speaking of Jesus as the 'Word'.

The 'Word' (Logos) is a term that John takes from native Hebrew thought. The Hebrew word for 'to speak' or 'to say' is 'Amar' and from this root form was derived the noun 'Memra', an Aramaic form which means 'Word'.

At the time of Christ the average Jew spoke Aramaic, which belonged to the same language group as Hebrew. Many of the Old Testament Scriptures were paraphrased into Aramaic and they were called Targums. It is from the Targums, which were very familiar to the Jewish people, that John draws his usage of 'Word'. The usage of 'Word' in the Targums came about as follows:

In the centuries leading up to the birth of Christ we have a time when the Jewish people were fascinated with the transcendence of God, being more focused on His distance and the differences between God and anything else. This was due, in part to the 'silence' of God from circa 400 BC onwards; something the Jewish people could not adequately explain. Their view of God as being transcendent and powerful (which was not sufficiently balanced by seeing Him as one that communicates and reaches out to people) was also fuelled by their vulnerability. The Roman Empire dominated the Jewish people, and Greek culture and thought also posed a threat. Making their God so high and far away was a way of trying to prove their God was greater and more powerful than others, despite their ongoing oppression. Because of this prevalent thinking, Jewish leaders made every effort to avoid anthropomorphism (God being spoken of in human terms), and when they found the Old Testament speaking of God in this way they substituted the language of anthropomorphism with 'the Word' in the Targums. An example of this is as follows:

'My own hand laid the foundations of the earth, and my right hand spread out the heavens…' (Isa. 48:13 The Bible).

'By My Word I have founded the earth, and by my strength I have hung up the heavens' (The Targum).

Professor Custance, in his book *The Trinity in the Old Testament* writes:

In the Targums they used this noun (Word) in many places where it seemed to them that God was spoken of as having direct and concrete dealings with the physical world. In the Targum of Onkelos it is used, for example in Genesis 3:8, 10, and 24. In verse eight, the text reads; "And they heard the voice of the Word (Memra) walking in the garden in the cool of the day." Even more striking in this Targum is the rendering of Deuteronomy 33:27 in which the words, "underneath are the everlasting arms," are replaced by the words "and by His Word was the world created." This is, of course exactly the thought in John 1:10 …. this term is substituted for the name of the Lord about 170 times in the Targum of Onkelos.'

From what has been related so far, it is easy to see that John knew exactly what he was saying when he called Jesus the 'Word'. In Jesus we see the Word of God made flesh – the Pre-Incarnate Son limiting Himself, humbling Himself and coming in the likeness of man so that we can have light and life instead of chaos and darkness. As Geoffrey Grogan writes:

He was one with us because divine power was channelled into his human life through the mediation of the Spirit (c.f. Luke 4:13 and Eph. 3:20). He was unlike us because the true source of this power was in his own divine being, while for us, the power of God is a gift of his grace, his favour, which we do not deserve (2 Cor 12). Incarnation (God becoming man) is the key to the first, indwelling (God living in man) the key to the second. This makes him truly human and yet truly divine (*What the Bible teaches about Jesus*, p. 123).

Jesus came as a man under the Law, whilst retaining Deity, so that we could come out from under condemnation and exchange rags for riches. Through Jesus we turn away from sin, and towards a loving and benevolent God, and it is in Jesus that we see the love and compassion, and the power and life of God in action within the limitations of the flesh. He was birthed into this world to save us. He did not think His riches were a treasure to be held on to – no, He limited Himself and lived for the Father, enabling us to enter into fellowship with God when we place our trust in Him.

God reveals Himself to us through revelation, since His realm is not present to our immediate perception. Apart from this, man's fall into sin means that (outside of Christ) we cannot approach God, who lives in unapproachable light (1 Tim 6:16). Yet because of God's love for us, He chose to communicate with fallen mankind, and God is the perfect communicator.

God is more than human, but since God is a person, God's being overlaps with ours as human beings, so that talk of God's 'love' and 'wrath' are true talk of God.... God's true revelation comes from out of itself to meet what we can say with our human words and make a selection from among them to which we have to attach ourselves in obedience' (J. Goldingay, *Models for Scripture*, p. 319).

Realising that God conveys eternal truth through the medium of language, and uses examples from life around us to help us understand truth at time, helps avoid the mistake of taking absolutely everything He says in a purely literal sense. For example, we could give an idea of how big a person is, by saying that he is 'as big as a house', yet no one would go around looking for a man with a roof on his head. Therefore, when Jesus says, 'I am the Vine', we understand that He does not mean He is literally a green plant bearing small round fruit. He is pointing out that, as the grapes are totally dependent on the Vine for sustenance, man's true sustenance is found only in Him. He is the true Vine (chiefly in contrast to the Judaism of the day, e.g. Ps. 80:8), and life is found in Him, not in any other religious leader or form of religious belief.

Similarly, such language as 'seated at the Father's right hand' (Heb. 8:1; 10:12) should not be taken literally, as is done by some who would try to use it to prove that Jesus is 'another god', or even just a prophet, but not God.

To say that Jesus is seated at God's right hand takes up the fact that a human king's son or regent would sit at the king's right hand and the consequent fact that the King of Israel was described as metaphorically seated at God's right. The image is then applied to God and Jesus. It does not mean that the Second Testament envisages two literal thrones in the sky with Quasi-human figures seated on them' (J. Goldingay, *Models for Scripture*, p. 322).

Another word that is worth looking at, in the light of what we have been saying is 'Son'.

Firstly, we note that the word 'Son', as applied to Jesus in relation to God, does not contain the physical meaning some assume it does. God is Spirit (John 4:24) and therefore 'Son' cannot refer to any physical relationship having taken place between God and Mary. John's first chapter clearly speaks of the pre-existence of Jesus (see also John 8:58). In coming to Mary (Luke 1:31-35) the Holy Spirit 'prepared a body' for the Pre-Incarnate Son, and so Jesus was birthed through the then virgin, Mary, having no need of a human father.

'Therefore, when Christ came into the world, he said: "Sacrifice and offering you did not desire, but a body you prepared for me"' (Heb. 10:5)

The word 'prepared' is from the Greek root 'katartizo' meaning 'to repair,' 'adjust,' 'mend,' and the picture we gain is of God repairing the DNA structure of an egg in the womb of Mary, prior to Christ's birth. Jesus did not put on flesh as one puts on a suit. He took flesh to Himself and became man, whilst retaining His Deity. He was man who did not need to die – the God-man, without even a hint of sin about Him. The belief that Jesus was a literal Son of God (through intercourse) comes from erroneous teaching circulating prior to the time of Mohammed. It was never a view that orthodox Christians held, and Scripture shows that the Jews were not offended by the term 'Son of God' as if they thought it meant that God produced a Son. However, what did cause offence amongst many Jews was Jesus' claim to be the Son of God in a unique sense. Both angels and believers are called 'sons of God' and Israel as a nation was called by God, 'my Son' (Gen. 6:2; Exod. 4:22, 23; Job 1:6). However, Jesus claimed to be the Son of God in a unique sense (Matt. 11:27; 21:37-38; 22:2; Mark 12:6; John 3:16; 5:19-23).

In John 1:18 Jesus is spoken of as 'God, the One and Only, who is at the Father's side,' and John 3:16 speaks of God's 'one and only Son'. Here, in looking at the Greek, we find the words 'one and only' coming from the Greek word 'monogenes,' meaning 'single of its kind only', 'only begotten'. The reason that John uses this particular word is because it implies that Jesus is not just a creature. A simple illustration helps us get the point.

When you make something, it can be very different from yourself – such as making a car or building a house. But the idea behind the word 'monogones,' is that of bringing about something which can only be the same as yourself. For

THE WORD OF GOD, ...

example a man and a woman produce human children, and birds produce eggs, which turn into birds, and so on. Hence John conveys the deity of Christ in the use of this word.' We then combine this with John's Jewish roots and find that the Semitic and oriental ideas of likeness, or sameness of nature, and equality of being, are always implied in the usage of the terms Father and Son. The title 'Son' given to the Second Person of the Trinity is not given to signify temporal derivation from the Father, but to signify His obedience to the will of the Father in becoming incarnate in our humanity. In doing this He is able to meet the claims of the Law and fulfil His purpose in redemption. The uniqueness of Jesus' sonship can also seen from such scriptures as Matthew 11:27:

'All things have been committed to me by my Father. No-one knows the Son except the Father, and no-one knows the Father except the Son and those to whom the Son chooses to reveal him.'

Professor G. Clark, commenting on the above verse, points out that the knowledge that the Father has of the Son is complete, divine and eternal. Therefore the same must be said of the knowledge that the Son has of the Father, since Jesus puts His knowledge on the same level as His Father's ('Trinity,' p. 14).

Jesus claimed equality with God (John 5:16-18), for which the Jews tried to stone Him, and yet,

JESUS CHRIST OR MOHAMMED?

in speaking of the Father he says, 'The Father is greater than I', since He willingly took a lower position for a season. Those who use 'the Father is greater than I' to disprove the Deity of Jesus fail to consider, at the very least, two points. Firstly, two brothers can work for a company in different positions, one a floor sweeper and the other an office manager. One may have a different position, but out of the work place one does not rule the other, and both are equal in essence. Jesus took a position for a season, and it is from this position of service that He speaks of the Father as 'greater than I.' Secondly, no prophet, would ever compare himself with God, suggesting quite clearly, that Jesus is far more than just a prophet.

On one occasion Jesus was called a 'good teacher' (Mark 10:17-18). In His reply to this Jesus says: 'Why do you call me good? "No-one is good – except God alone."' In His reply we do not find the words 'I am not good' which some opponents to His Deity would have us believe. Instead we have Deity clearly implied. If no-one is good except God, and Jesus has just been called 'good,' maybe the young man, who had just spoken to him, should put two and two together! Let us also remember, at this point, that no-one could accuse Jesus of any sin, He even challenged those closest to Him to find sin if they could.

Moving back to John 1:1, and drawing things to a conclusion, we now note a final point.

The Word was not God independently of His

union with the Father and the Holy Spirit.

He is God, in union with Father and Spirit, just as the Father Himself is not God except in union with the Son and the Holy Spirit, and so on. This can lead to the question: 'How can Christ be called "God" when he was not God except in union with the Father and the Holy Spirit?' Again we need to look back to the usage of language. The answer is found in that God speaks to us in our own language and uses our idioms. Take the following as an example: You and I use the term 'man', when speaking only of his body, his soul, and his spirit, to indicate his species – that he is a human being, not an animal, an angel or a spirit. We say, 'he is a tall man', speaking only of his body; 'he is a clever man' speaking only of his soul; and 'he is a godly man' with reference only to his spirit, his differentia from animals. Then again, with reference to food we say, 'I have eaten a banana', when we have only eaten a part of it, not the skin, and of an orange, when we have not eaten of the rind. It is in this sense of distinguishing the nature of His being, as divine, not a creature, that Christ as Son of God, is called 'God.' It is in this way that we would also call the Father 'God,' and the Holy Spirit 'God.' The title is given to them individually to reveal that they are not created Beings, but each share equally in the one Divine differentiated life. Thus the term 'Father', like 'Son' and 'Spirit', distinguishes them from each other (as 'spirit', 'soul' and 'body' distinguishes each part of our being from each other), whilst speaking of the One God.

In Jesus we have the speech of eternity translated into the actions of time; dare we even say it, God made simple. In Jesus, God stoops low to lift up those who deserve nothing but death. From what we have seen, one thing is certain. He is God Incarnate. He did not come in all glory and power, but within the limitations of humanity, this being the only way of bringing a lost people back to God. One day He will return – and then we shall see Him as He is, whether we like it or not.

The Cry of Dereliction?
'My God, My God, why have you forsaken me.' The above verse has often been put forward by those who wish to deny the Deity of Christ as 'rock-solid' proof that Jesus is not God. As shall now be seen, this verse proves nothing of the sort.

In both Gospels (Matt. 27:46 and Mark 15:34) the words 'My God, My God, why have you forsaken me' are intentionally preserved in Aramaic and Hebrew to draw our attention to the fact that Christ is quoting a portion of the Old Testament in His cry. Jesus is not questioning God as if He needed an answer to His cry. If He had thought God had totally abandoned Him, He would not have used the word 'My' before 'God,' or later said, 'Father, into your hands I commit my Spirit' (Luke 23:46). Instead of questioning God, Jesus is giving us an idea of what He is going

THE WORD OF GOD, ...

through by quoting scripture that furnishes us with information.

In these words Jesus is quoting Psalm 22:1, which is a part of a Psalm speaking of a sufferer undergoing great opposition from those around him for no valid reason whatsoever. However the Psalmist's trust in God does not fail – hence the words 'MY God, MY God, why have you forsaken me?' He may feel alone and separated, but still knows that God is His God, and as the Psalm later reveals it is God who rescues Him – for He has done no wrong. Those steeped in the Hebrew scriptures would understand that in quoting this Psalm, Jesus is revealing that it speaks of Him as an innocent man before His enemies. His cry therefore expresses something of the separation He was going through. However we must realise that this separation is not a separation of Being, but a cessation of fellowship and communication. Jesus was paying the price for our sins. It had always been His intention to give His life for us, and He willingly chose to walk that path (Luke 22:24). Jesus had made His decision, and it was impossible for Him to do anything but remain as a willing sacrifice for our sins.

There are those who state that Jesus' cry proves that He is not God. Yet as already noted it was not a cry of despair so much as a cry of communication, informing us of something of the horror of what was going on, yet also revealing His absolute control over the situation. As the following pale illustrations reveal, it is possible to become separated from most of the thinking that makes us us, whilst still being very much present. For example, if you or I were to see a man step out in front of us and slowly slit his throat with a large knife, the sight of it would 'separate' us from anything else we were thinking about at the time. Communion with self would cease, although all our thoughts were still within us. We may even be paralysed with fear, and the shock of that moment might suspend everything else so that we were, in a sense, isolated from all around and within us (save that which we faced), even if only for just a split second. Yet we are still all there. In a very pale way this helps us understand that Jesus is not saying that God is not present to Him any more, after all He is God Incarnate. But there is silence. The judgement time of sin had arrived and the forsaking of internal communication is spoken of, indicating the judgement of God (Father, Son and Spirit) on all sin. Yet the written word is held onto, indicating a powerful truth. All is not lost.

Another pale illustration may be of help. Imagine that you were going to climb in the Arctic. You plan your route meticulously, and mark your map and work out all the compass bearings. Then you begin to climb. The mist comes in and it begins to snow, and visibility decreases to just a few inches. Your mind totally focuses on your compass bearing and nothing else occupies your thoughts. The noise of the blizzard, the howling wind, lack of visibility and lack of feeling in parts of your body, make it seem as if you have abandoned your senses – as if the rest of you is not really there. However you are still very much present – body, soul and spirit. The single thought and focus of your mind – remembering the map and compass bearing – does not deny the existence, or presence, of the rest of you. Lack of interaction with the rest of your thinking processes does not make you think that the rest of you is not there!

Jesus had come to do a job. He had come to pay the price for our sins. There was no need for communication within Trinitarian unity at this time. Indeed there could be no communication because the wrath of God was upon the sacrifice. God does not look upon sin and there is no focus on it in any way – only judgement. Therefore at judgement, the one undergoing our penalty speaks the written word – recalling what had been recorded in the past, focusing upon truth, since there could be no focus on sin. The words communicate the agony and yet express the perfect truth – a trust in God, an awareness that the victim is innocent, and the certain hope which the Psalmists expressed, is translated into the words: 'Father, into your hands I commit my Spirit.'

The Witness of other Apostles to Christ
The Acts of the Apostles
In the Acts of the Apostles we find the title 'kurios' (Lord) given as often to Christ as to the

Father. The word 'kurios' is used to translate 'Jehovah' (God) in the Greek Old Testament. Because of the judgement God pronounced on all who used His name irreverently, the Jews substituted 'Adonai' for 'Jehovah.' Therefore the Hebrew text of Psalm 110:1 reads 'Adonai said to Adoni.' Those who later translated the Hebrew into Greek translated both Adonai and Adoni by kurios, realising that both meant Jehovah God. Concerning Psalm 110:1 it is only God who could be David's Lord!

1. For the application of kurios to Christ, see Acts 2:36; 4:33; 5:14; 7:59-60; 9:5, 6, 10, 11, 13, 17; 10:36, 48; 11:16, 17, 21, 23, 24; 12:11; 13:2, 11, 12; 13:23; 15:11, 17, 26; 16:31, 32; 18:5, 25; 19:10; 20:9, 21, 34, 35; 21:13, 14; 23:11; 26:15; 28:31.

2. Some critics assert that kurios is Hellenistic and could not therefore have been given to Christ by Palestinian writers. This is refuted by the fact that in 1 Corinthians 16:22 Paul used the Aramaic 'Marana tha' (Our Lord come).

   a. It is Jesus Christ who bestows the gift of the Holy Spirit to His believing people (Acts 2:33). Even if the Holy Spirit had been only a Divine influence (which has already been shown to be false), no created being could have bestowed it on others.

   b. Divine names are applied to the Spirit. The language of Jehovah in the Old Testament is represented in the New Testament as the language of the Holy Spirit. For example, compare Exodus 17:7, and Psalm 95:7 with Hebrews 3:7-11. Also compare Isaiah 6:9 with Acts 28:25, and Jeremiah 31:31, 33, 34 with Hebrews 10:15. If he is never called 'God' (theos) directly, He is indirectly (Acts 5:3, 4; 1 Cor. 3:16-17; 6:19; Eph. 2:22).

c. Divine attributes are ascribed to the Holy Spirit. He is revealed as omnipresent (everywhere present) in 1 Corinthians 12:13, and Psalm 139:7. He is revealed as omniscient (all knowing) in 1 Corinthians 2:10-11, and omnipotent (all powerful) in Luke 1:35 and Romans 8:21.

d. Divine nature is His, the only unpardonable sin being blasphemy against the Holy Spirit (Matt. 12:31, 32).

e. Divine works such as creation (Gen. 1:2; Job 26:13; Ps. 104:30) are performed by the Holy Spirit. The Holy Spirit also enables faith, without eliminating free will. He convicts people of sin, righteousness and judgement, and applies the work of Christ to those who choose to repent (John 3:5; 6:44; Acts 7:51; 1 Cor. 6:11; 2 Thess. 2:13; 1 Pet. 1:2; 1 Thess. 4:3).

f. In the baptismal formula (Matt. 28:19) and the apostolic benediction (2 Cor. 13:13, 14), He is coequally with the Father and the Son the object of faith and worship.

g. His offices clearly reveal His Divine Person. He is Teacher, Guide, Comforter and Advocate. He is the Helper and Intercessor, the Enlightener and Sanctifier of the whole Church as well as of individual believers (Luke 12:12; Acts 5:32; 15:28; 16:6; 28:25; Rom. 8:2, 14-26; 15:15; 1 Cor. 2:13; 3:16; 12:3-13; 2 Cor. 3:17, 18; Eph. 3:5,16; 2 Thess. 2:13; Heb. 2:4; 3:7; 2 Pet. 1:21).

3. It is important to understand the distinction which Scripture makes between the Person of the Holy Spirit and His influence. When the influence of the Spirit is being referred to, there is the absence of the article (the word 'the') before 'Spirit'. Therefore passages that refer to the baptism, outpouring and in-filling of the Spirit refer to His influence. Some cults, such as the Jehovah's Witnesses, use these Scriptures referring to the Holy Spirit as an influence to prove He is not a person. However they fail to take into consideration Scriptures which prove that the Holy Spirit is the Person whose influence is referred to! For example, in John 14:16–16:7-14 Christ refers to the Person of the Holy Spirit by use of personal pronouns. In the Upper Room on His resurrection day, He refers to the influence of the Spirit, speaking of the 'power' coming to indwell them, saying

'receive you Holy Spirit' there is no article before Spirit (John 20:22). Ephesians 5:18 also speaks of the influence of the Spirit in saying 'Keep on being filled with Spirit.' For further examples of the article when it is His Person which is referred to, see 1 Corinthians 2:11, 14; 3:16; 6:11, 19.

4. In the Apostles preaching, Jesus stands in the place of God as Saviour in the Old Testament. Note: Isaiah 1:18-20; 41:14; 43:11, 25; 44:6, 22, 24; 45:21, 22; 46:13; 47:4; 48:17; 49:7, 26; 54:5, 6; 60:16; 63:16; Jeremiah 50:34. In Isaiah 59:20 and 62:11, 12, Messiah is called the Redeemer of Israel. Sinners receive salvation only through faith in Jesus Christ (Acts 4:12; 2:38; 5:31; 13:38, 39)

5. Jesus is addressed in prayer (Acts 7:59; 9:13, 14, 21; 22:16). Many commentators believe that Jesus is referred to in Acts 1:24 because it is He who is referred to in verse 21.

6. Jesus is the Judge of all (Acts 10:42; 17:31). See Genesis 18:25; Exodus 12:12; Psalm 58:11; Isaiah 33:22. Messiah is called the 'Judge of Israel' in Micah 5:1.

7. Jesus is the Prince of Life (Acts 3:15). See Psalm 26:9; Jeremiah 2:13.

8. In Acts 3:14; 7:52; 22:14, the title given to Jesus is 'The Righteous One.' The particular reference here is not to His Deity, but to His perfect righteousness as Man. The Law, as we have seen, demanded perfect human

righteousness as the condition of justification and of eternal life (Matt. 19:16,17; Lev. 18:5). By His perfect obedience to its commandments Christ obtained this righteousness for us and eternal life as free gifts to faith (Rom 5:17; 6:23). His perfect righteousness as Man was also necessary to the union of Deity with humanity in Him.

9. In Acts 20:28 Paul admonishes the elders assembled at Miletus to 'feed the Church of God, which He purchased with His own blood'. Here again the Person of Christ as incarnate Deity is asserted, since a comparison with other references to the church as 'the church of God' speaks out against other interpretations (1 Cor. 1:2; 2:1; 10:32; 11:16; 1 Tim. 3:15; Gal. 1:13).

10. 'Keep watch over yourselves and all the flock of which the Holy Spirit has made you overseers. Be shepherds of the church of God, which he brought with his own blood.' The Deity of Christ is clearly seen in the above verse. The verse reveals that His blood was not only the medium through which He revealed as man His perfect obedience to the Law of Love at the supremest cost, the blood was also the medium through which His incarnate Deity revealed the love of God in its supreme sacrifice in His bearing God's judgement on the sin of the world.

Paul's letter to the Romans

Christ was charged by the Jews with claiming to be God incarnate, coequal with God. Jesus never denied that He had made these claims, and was crucified for this apparent 'blasphemy'. His resurrection, Paul says in Romans 1:1-4, showed that every claim that Christ had made was true, and that He was indeed God incarnate. Like Christ Himself, Paul makes the resurrection the proof of His being the Messiah of Old Testament prophecy – the Son of God incarnate in the Son of David, the Child born, the Son given, whose name would be called 'The Wonderful Counsellor, the Mighty God, the Creator of a New Age, the Prince of Peace,' Emmanuel, God with us, the world's sin-bearer and Redeemer (Isa. 9:6; 7:14; 53).

In Romans 9:5 we read: 'Of whom (Israel) are the fathers, and of whom as concerning the flesh Christ came, who is over all, God blessed for ever and ever.' The words 'as concerning the flesh Christ came' are another reference to His supernatural birth, no natural birth ever being so described.

We also note that the titles 'Lord' and 'God' are interchangeable and apply to both the Father and Christ in Romans 14:6.

Trinity in the benedictions

Paul unites the Son with the Father so closely, and with the Holy Spirit, that only their unity of being in the One Godhead can explain it. The Trinity is clearly revealed in the benediction; 'The grace of our Lord Jesus Christ, and the love of God, and the fellowship of the Holy Spirit, be with you all, Amen' (2 Cor. 13:14). The same, or equivalent greetings, are found in 2 Corinthians 1:2; Galatians 1:3; Philippians 1:2; Colossians 1:2; 2 Thessalonians 1:1, 2; Titus 1:4; Philemon 1:3. The name Mohammed is never linked with Allah in this way, nor Plato's with Zeus.

Titus 2:13

'… while we wait for the blessed hope – the glorious appearing of our great God and Saviour, Jesus Christ' (Titus 2:13).

There are those who would say that the above verse speaks of two people, since the word 'and' must unite two different persons. However, these critics need to note the following:-

1. There is only one article in the construction. The text does not read: 'the glorious appearing of our great God and THE Saviour, Jesus Christ.'
2. In many passages we have 'our God and Father,' where all agree 'Father' is not a different person from 'God.' For example, Philippians 4:20 reads: 'To our God and Father be glory forever and ever. Amen.' Other examples include 1 Thessalonians 3:11 and 2 Corinthians 11:31.

3. To interpret 'Our God and Father' as speaking of one Person, and yet to interpret 'Our great God and Saviour Jesus Christ' as speaking of two is therefore seen as wrong. This erroneous view arise from the presupposition that the Divine Unity must be mathematical. As we have already seen in this book, the belief in the Deity of Christ does not cancel the belief in the unity of God. In the mind of all the churches, Trinitarianism was the only true form of Monotheism.

James

In James 2:1 Christ is called, with reference to His Deity, 'the Lord of Glory.' which no created being can ever be!

There are, of course, many other scriptures throughout the New Testament which clearly reveal the Deity of Christ.

16

The Witness of Paul

There are many Muslim writers who would have us believe that Christianity is no more than the invention of Paul, and that he did not hold true to any of Christ's teaching. In light of this we note the following points, which easily show the error of these writers.

1. Paul testifies that before his conversion he was one of the greatest opponents of the Church. At a later stage he writes to Galatian Christians saying: 'For you have heard of my previous way of life in Judaism, how intensely I persecuted the church of God, and tried to destroy it' (Gal. 1:13). In Acts 26:11 we read that he went from synagogue to synagogue to have Christians punished, and to make them blaspheme. The Christians believed that Jesus was God Incarnate, which, as a zealous Jew, Paul did not accept. To him this was blasphemy, and getting them to blaspheme was all the fuel he needed to seek to destroy them. From this we see that the deity of Christ was not a Pauline invention.

2. In 1 Corinthians 15:3-8 Paul gives a list of eye-witnesses to the resurrection of Christ, which he states took place on the third day 'according to Scripture.' This tells us that, at the very least, one Gospel was so well known that he could appeal to it as evidence for those who did not believe him. This alone, clearly reveals that Paul did not invent the resurrection of Christ from the dead!

3. When we look at the lengths that Paul went to, in order to destroy Christians, we are left asking a question. What could have happened to make him change in such a way?

4. His unparalleled sufferings for Christ, and the complete sacrifice of everything that he held dear to him (2 Cor. 11:23-31; Phil. 3:7-10), can only be explained by the fact that Paul met with the risen Christ.

5. There were many Christians prior to Paul's conversion, who were still very present on the world scene after his conversion. Yet we hear of none ever writing that Paul changed the central truths of Christianity to suit his own purposes. Instead, we see his enemies coming against him for holding exactly the same beliefs that had initially caused Paul to persecute Christians.

6. There is only one satisfactory explanation as to why Paul sacrificed all that he had prized in Judaism and went through unparalleled suffering for Christ (2 Cor. 11:23-31; Phil. 3:7-10). All of this was a result of meeting

the risen Christ on the road to Damascus
(Acts 22:1-16; 26:1-18).

7. Concerning the above event, we note that
devout Jews were travelling with him at the
time (Acts 9:1-22). These men would have
returned to the Sanhedrin to explain why
Paul had abandoned his mission. There are no
records of anyone denying Paul's experience,
or proving it to be false.

8. It is impossible for Paul to have changed the
message of Christ. Christ said that the whole
purpose of his mission was to fulfil the Law
(Matt. 5:17), and this is what Paul does
(Rom. 3:19–5:21; 8:3; Gal. 3-5:6; Phil 3:7-9).
This Law makes such a Saviour as Christ
essential if sinners are to be saved, and certain
because it reveals that God is love. God's Law
of love tests Paul's doctrine, and proves it to be
the true doctrine of Christ.

9. In preaching at Antioch in Pisidia
(Acts 13:22-39), Paul proclaims the risen Jesus
of Nazareth to be the Messiah of Israel and
only Saviour of sinners. He points out that the
prophecies of the Messiah's lineage, death as an
atonement for sin, and resurrection, were all
fulfilled completely in Him. Comparing this
message (Acts 13:22-39) with Peter's sermon
on the Day of Pentecost (Acts 2:22-39;
3:12-26) clearly reveals that they preached the
same message.

10. A man who suffered so greatly for Christ,

JESUS CHRIST OR MOHAMMED?

without any prospect of earthly gain, could not have been an impostor. Paul was an academic in the field of Judaism, and a leader and teacher of others. On accepting Christ his life shows none of the peculiarities one would expect from a lunatic who lived out his delusions. Instead, we see a man who was calm and rational and continuously reaching towards others in good works, yet denying that they had any merit at all concerning his salvation, because he trusted completely in the saving work of Jesus Christ.

11. At the council of Jerusalem (Acts 15) we see that the church willingly accepted Paul's testimony concerning how the Gentiles were saved by placing their trust in Jesus alone. The church would hardly have accepted this testimony if Paul had been preaching a message contrary to the teachings of Christ.

12. Both of Peter's letters reveal that his doctrine of the Person and Work of Christ are in perfect agreement with Paul's. He refers to Paul as 'our beloved brother' and calls his writings 'Scriptures' (2 Pet. 3:15-16).

17

The Resurrection of Christ

There are those who believe that differences in the accounts of the resurrection of Christ prove that it never happened. Yet differences in accounts by different reporters are not evidences to contradiction, or that the event never happened. Imagine, for example, that two people write about me parking my car in my drive one night. The first person writes: 'The two headlights dazzled me as he parked his car,' whilst the second writer states, 'I saw two red lights glowing extra brightly, as he parked his car.' It would not be very clever to say the event never occurred just because the accounts were different! One man was standing in front of the car as I parked it, whilst one was behind the car, seeing the brake-lights go on.

In the eighteenth century in this country two men who did not believe in the resurrection of Christ or in His deity planned to launch an attack on the Christian faith that would end it once and for all. Their names were Lord Lyttleton, K.C., and his friend Gilbert West. Since the resurrection of Christ is the foundation stone of Christianity, Gilbert West undertook to write a book to prove, from supposed contradictions, that the resurrection never happened. Lord Lyttleton undertook to disprove the scriptural accounts of Paul's conversion, which, as the record stands, is so great an evidence for the resurrection of Christ. They arranged to meet together the following year to report the progress of their undertakings. Each was rather concerned at what the effect of their report might be on the other as the result of their study was the exact opposite of what they had intended. Imagine, therefore, the great surprise and rejoicing when each reported they were convinced of the truthfulness of the scriptural records, and were to publish books defending the very scriptures they had set out to destroy.

In our own day, Frank Morrison also intended to write a book disproving the resurrection of Christ. But as a result of his study he wrote a book attesting the irrefutable fact of it, entitled *Who Moved the Stone?*

Only absolutely irrefutable evidence could have led avowed unbelievers in the resurrection of Christ to become wholly convinced believers in it. What prevents religious people from accepting the truths of Scripture is often the personal cost of doing so!

The apostles themselves all disbelieved, despite repeated predictions that Christ would rise from the dead the third day (Matt. 17:19; Mark 8:31;

10:33, 34; 14:27, 28, Luke 18:31-33). They also disbelieved the message of the women disciples to whom Jesus appeared first; they were the originators of the 'hallucination theory'. What stronger testimony to the fact that Christ publicly claimed that He would rise from the dead the third day could any unbelievers ask for than the testimony of the Sanhedrin to Pilate? Their request for a guard of Roman soldiers was to prevent the disciples stealing away His body by night. The non-denial of the record of their request is found in Matthew 27:63, 64.

Another point worth noting is this: What forger would dream of stating that Christ first appeared to Mary of Magdala? (Mark 16:9; John 30:1-18). Why not use John or Peter or Mary of Bethany instead? Apart from this, no forger would state that the apostles did not believe Christ's predictions.

One harmonising of the Gospel accounts, proving that they do not contradict each other, was done by George Eldon Ladd; whose work I use below:

1. The earthquake and the removal of the stone before dawn.
2. Very early on a group of four women come to the tomb wondering who will remove the stone. As they approach, they are amazed to see that the stone has been rolled away.
3. Mary rushes off to tell Peter and John that the body of Jesus has been stolen (John 20:2).

4. The other women stay in the garden. They enter the tomb and are met by two angels, who tell them to carry the word of the resurrection to the disciples. The problem of a 'young man' of Mark 16:5, 'two men' of Luke 24:4 and 'angels' of Luke 24:23 is one of ordinary synoptic divergences of detail. (For example, stating that there were two men would only make the account of one man be wrong if it stated 'there were only ever two men there,' which is not stated. Brackets mine.)

5. The women rush away from the garden, filled with mingled emotions of fear and joy, speaking to no one about the vision of the angels at the empty tomb (Mark 16:8).

6. Later in the day, Jesus met them (Matt. 28:9 does not say this meeting occurred in the garden). They had run away from the tomb. Jesus tells them to bear the word to the disciples; they depart to find the disciples, who are not together, but scattered (Matt. 28:9-10).

7. Peter and John, having been informed by Mary, come to the tomb after the women have left. They see the clothes; vague comprehension dawns on John. They rush off to gather the disciples.

8. Mary returns to the tomb after Peter and John have left, they run to the tomb leaving Mary behind. She still thinks the body of Jesus has been stolen. She is weeping outside the tomb, knowing nothing of the experience

of the women she had left in the garden. She sees the two angels, then Jesus (John 20:11-17). (Mark 16:9-20 is omitted from the oldest MSS).

9. After the first shock of amazement had worn off, the women find some of the disciples; the disciples cannot believe the fanciful story (Luke 24:11).

10. The disciples have gathered together.

11. Mary arrives and tells her experience (John 20:18).

12. That afternoon they walk to Emmaus (Luke 24:13-33).

13. Sometime that afternoon, an appearance to Peter (Luke 24:34).

14. That evening the disciples are all together in the closed room. They had been scattered, but the testimony of the women, of Peter and John, and then of Mary, serves to bring them together. Thomas was absent (Luke 24:33-46; John 20:19-23).

15. A second appearance to the eleven, including Thomas (John 20:26-29).

16. Galilee (Matt. 28:16).

17. The appearance by Tiberius (John 21), and to the 500 people (1 Cor. 15:6).

18. Return to Jerusalem; the final appearance and ascension.

Ladd goes on to state that no evangelist sought to give a complete history of the appearances of

Christ. His harmonisation is not intended to suggest that events must have happened in this order.

The Genealogies of Jesus in Matthew and Luke

In his efforts to discredit the testimonies of the Gospels to Christ, Dr Bucaille, a Moslem scholar, says that the two accounts are contradictory, and so disproves the claim that they are the word of God. However, Jewish contemporaries obviously did not see any contradictions since they did not bring this objection against the New Testament writers.

Luke gives the genealogy of Jesus through Mary, and Matthew gives it through Joseph.

In Matthew we are told that Joseph was the son of Jacob (Matt. 1:16) whilst Luke says Joseph was the son of Heli (Luke 3:23). He could not by natural generation be both the son of Jacob and the son of Heli. The solution is easily seen in that Joseph was the son-in-law of Heli, who was, like himself, a descendent of David. That he should be called the son of Heli would be in accordance with Jewish usage (see 1 Sam. 24:16). The conclusion is therefore inevitable that in Luke we have the genealogy of Mary; and Joseph was the 'son of Heli' because espoused to the daughter of Heli. The genealogy in Luke is Mary's, whose father, Heli, was descended from David.

Whilst looking in the area of supposed contradictions we note that some reject the Bible as the Word of God because John contradicts the other Gospels' date of Christ's eating the last Passover with His disciples. The simple answer to this is that the Sadducees, who took the leading part in the crucifixion of Jesus, celebrated the Passover the day after the Pharisees, the 15th of Nisan. When John uses the words 'before the Feast of the Passover' (John 13:1), he is referring to the Sadducean date for observing it.

The Day of Christ's Crucifixion

For many years it has been the conviction of many Bible students that our Lord was crucified on the Wednesday of what people term Holy Week, and not on the Friday. On this subject Dr R.A. Torrey wrote nearly a hundred years ago in *Difficulties in the Bible*:

It is said that Jesus was crucified on 'The day before the Sabbath' (Mark 15:42). As the Jewish weekly Sabbath came on Saturday, beginning at sunset the evening before, the conclusion is naturally drawn that He must have been crucified on the Friday. But it is a well-known fact to which the Bible bears abundant testimony that the Jews had other Sabbaths beside the weekly Sabbath, which fell on Saturday. The first day of the Passover week, no matter on what day of the week it came, was always a Sabbath (Exod. 12:16; Num. 28:16-18). The question therefore arises whether the Sabbath which followed Christ's crucifixion was the weekly Sabbath or the

Passover Sabbath, falling on the 15th Nissan which came that year on a Thursday. Now the Bible does not leave us to speculate in regard to which Sabbath is meant in this instance, for John in so many words tells us in John 19:14, that the day on which Jesus was tried and crucified was 'the preparation of the Passover', that is, the day before the Passover Sabbath, which came that year on a Thursday.

More recently, Dr D. G. Barnhouse wrote:

I personally have always held that there were two Sabbaths in our Lord's last week – the Saturday Sabbath, and the Passover Sabbath, the latter being on Thursday. They hastened to take his body down after a Wednesday crucifixion, and He was three days and three nights in the tomb (at least 72 hours), arising from the dead shortly after sunset on the first day of the week (the equivalent of Saturday evening about 7 pm under our modern way of reckoning).

When I was a young man in my early twenties. I discovered the truth about Christianity, having previously judged it as outdated, irrelevant, and of little value to twentieth century society. Through meeting Christians and examining the claims of Christianity I came to see that there was a God who created this world and placed man within it, so that man could benefit from His love and serve Him. In this, I found that life had meaning and purpose after all. I also came to see, as many millions of people before me had seen, that man is a sinner who has transgressed God's perfect law of love. I also saw that God is holy and perfect and that no amount of good works give any man the right to stand before Him. Yet, I was also made aware of a Saviour – Jesus Christ – who loved me and gave His life so that I could come out from condemnation and into a living relationship with God as my heavenly Father. I asked God to forgive my sins and asked Jesus to be my Lord and Saviour, recognising that He had paid the full price for my sins at Calvary, and risen victorious from the grave.

In Jesus I found one who has such power and yet is so gentle; one who is so holy, not tolerating my sinful ways, yet one who also stoops low to lift me up when I fail. Yet in Jesus I have found one who challenges me. He challenges me to love others as I myself am loved by Him, and this is why you have this book in your hand.

Many of us are challenged by the problems and difficulties in the world around us, and react against others who do not hold the same view, or live a different way. Yet this book was not produced to be a reaction against a different religion. It came about through a challenge from the One True God – and that challenge was, as it always will be, to love others. This book has been produced so that men and women may be able to catch a brief glimpse of the truth concerning Christ who is the light of the world. In doing this, I sincerely hope and pray that men and women may come to that place where they can make an informed decision to place their lives in the hands of a living Saviour. If you want to find out more about Jesus, then please read the Bible, and ask the One True God to open your heart and mind as you do so. Thank you.

Acknowledgements

Alexander, W.L, *Christ and Christianity.* Jackson and Walford, London (1853).

Anderson, Prof. J, *The Bible - The Word of God.*

Anderson, Prof. N, *The Inadequacy of Non-Christian Religions.* IVP (1944).

Baillie, D.M, *God was in Christ.* Faber & Faber, London (1947).

Brace, C.L, *The Unknown God.* Hodder & Stoughton (1889).

Bruce, A.B, *The Humiliation of Christ,* T & T Clark, Edinburgh (1881).

Butrus, Archpriest Zachariah, *God is One in the Holy Trinity.* Private Publications.

Chadwick, Dr G.A, *The Expositor's Bible – Gospel of Mark.* Hodder & Stoughton (1887).

Clark, Prof. G, *Trinity.* Trinity Foundation (1984).

Custance, A, *Trinity in the Old Testament.* Doorway Papers (1951).

Custance, A, *Who taught Adam to Speak?* Doorway Papers (1961).

Dods, Dr. Marcus, *The Atonement in Modern Thought,* Lutterworth Press, Cambridge (1901).

Fisher, G.P, *History of Christian Doctrine.* T & T Clark, Edinburgh (1985).

Forrest, D.W, *The Christ of History and Experience.* T & T Clark, Edinburgh (1890).

Franks, Dr. R.S, *The History of the Doctrine of the Work of Christ.* Hodder & Stoughton (1951).

Goldingnay, Prof. J, *Models for Scripture.* Eerdmans (1994).

Grogan, G, *What the Bible Teaches about Jesus*. Tyndale Press (1979).

Illingworth, Dr, *The Doctrine of the Trinity*. McMillan (1897).

John, S.B, *The Finality of Christ*. Kingsgate Press, London.

Kennedy, W, *The Self Revelation of Jesus*. Ibister Ltd, London.

Knowling, Dr, *Messianic Interpretations*. SPCK, London (1910).

Ladd, G.E, *I believe in the Resurrection of Jesus*. Hodder & Stoughton (1974-5).

Lang, Dr. J. Marshall, *The Last Supper*. Hodder & Stoughton (1888).

Lapide, Dr. Pinchas, *Erroneous Translations*. SPCK, London.

Lapide, Dr. Pinchas, *The Resurrection of Jesus*. SPCK, London (1984).

Liddon, H.P, *The Divinity of our Lord*. Longman Group (1890).

Manson, W, *Jesus the Messiah*. Hodder & Stoughton (1943).

McDowell, J, *Evidence That Demands a Verdict*. Here's Life Publications (1972).

Muir, Sir. William, *The Koran*. SPCK, London (1860).

Orr, J, *The Resurrection of Jesus*. Hodder & Stoughton (1908).

Paton, *Jesus Christ and World Religions*. Edinburgh House Press (1916).

Pfander, C.G, *Balance of Truth*. Light of Life (1986).

Philips, Dr. T, *The Grace of God and World Religions*, Baptist Union, London.

Pierson, Dr. A.T, *Difficulties in the Bible*. Richard Dickenson, London (1891).

Pratney, W, *Nature and Character of God*. Bethany House (1988).

Rhodes, R, *Christ Before the Manger*. Baker (1992).

Robinson, J.A.T, *Redating the New Testament*. SCM Press, London (1993).

Stobart, Principal, R. *Islam*. SPCK, London.

Storrs, R. *Many Creeds - One Christ,* Lutterworth Press, Cambridge.

Sweetman, Dr. J.W, *Islam and Christianity,* Lutterworth Press, Cambridge (1945).

Torrey, Dr. C.C, *Our Translated Gospel*. Harper & Co, New York (1937).

la Touche, Dr. Diggles, *The Person of Christ in Modern Thought,* Lutterworth Press, Cambridge (1890).

A *Muslim's* Pocket Guide To

Christianity

Malcolm Steer

A Muslims Pocket Guide to Christianity
Malcolm Steer

Relations between Muslims and Christians have been tested in recent years, with misunderstandings on both sides. To improve relations there needs to be a clearer picture of what each actually believes.

Christians don't always realise that a Muslim's view of their faith is often coloured by connotations of The Crusades, invasion, imperialism, immorality and blasphemy. Muslims don't always realise that believing Christians' core beliefs are centred on forgiveness, love and compassion.

Malcolm Steer, a Christian who has lived for many years amongst Muslims, has produced an accessible, straightforward and informative introduction to the Christian faith, looking at the origins, central beliefs and teachings of Christianity.

For any Muslim who seeks to discover more about Christianity this is an ideal book, enabling the reader to separate truth from myth and make an informed opinion.

ISBN 184550 1071

A Christian's Pocket Guide to

Islam

Patrick Sookhdeo

A Christian's Pocket Guide To Islam
Patrick Sookhdeo

Have you ever watched a T.V. programme or read a newspaper article where a commentator clumsily illustrates his complete ignorance of Christianity and it's claims? How often have you rolled your eyes and immediately discounted what is being said, saying to yourself "Well, why should I listen to them when they obviously haven't got a clue!" How, then, can we expect to witness effectively to those of the Muslim faith if all that we know of Islam is picked up from passing references in the media?

This fascinating book provides Christians with a simple description of the origins of Islam, what Muslims believe and how it affects their attitudes, worldview, everyday life and culture. Practical guidelines are given for relating to Muslims in a culturally appropriate way, as well as for witnessing effectively and caring for converts.

If you long to reach Muslim friends but are wondering where to start then this is the book for you.

'...clearly and concisely describes the major facets of that faith and is punctuated with helpful insights for those seeking positive ways to relate as Christian witnesses to Muslims.'
Rev. Dr Bill Musk, author of three books on Christians relating to Muslims

'Written for those with no prior knowledge of Islam, this book gives all the basic facts which will help a Christian to be more effective in their witness, as well as helpful guidance on how to approach Muslims lovingly and appropriately.'
Zafar Ismail, Chairman Interserve's Ministry Among Asians in Britain

Patrick Sookhdeo is Director of the Institute for the Study of Islam and Christianity, a Christian research institute specialising in the status of Christian minorities in the Muslim world.

ISBN 1 85792 699 4

Evangelistic

∨

A CHRISTIAN'S POCKET GUIDE

TO

islám

MALCOLM STEER

A Christian's Evangelistic Pocket Guide to Islam
Malcolm Steer

Speaking to Muslims about Christianity can be an unsettling experience for the Christian. Our understanding of the Muslim faith is very limited, and their critique of the Christian faith is often quite unlike any other we have come across. Despite the difficulties we are called to be ready to witness, and since Islam is the world's fastest growing religion, Christians everywhere are going to have to learn how to reach out to Muslims and answer their criticisms.

Malcolm Steer has a considerable amount of experience of witnessing to Muslims, he is familiar with their positions and shows how Christians can witness effectively. He shows how effective witnessing depends on:

1. Getting to Grips with Islam - having some knowledge of the beliefs and practices of Islam.
2. Getting the Message across - being aware of some of the misunderstandings that Muslims have about Christianity then knowing how to positively present the good news of Christ.
3. Getting the Approach right - that is, knowing how best to approach a Muslim.

Read this book and reach out to our Muslim neighbours and friends with confidence.

> *'This small booklet is something you **should not be without** if you want to be effective in your evangelism among Muslim people. A very useful tool, giving you knowledge, help and encouragement.'*
> **Dr. Elsie A. Maxwell**

Malcolm Steer lived in Iran for nine years and then for the past twenty years has been involved in a ministry to Iranians in the UK and Europe.

ISBN 1 85792 915 2

Christian Focus Publications
publishes books for all ages

Our mission statement –

STAYING FAITHFUL
In dependence upon God we seek to help make His infallible Word, the Bible, relevant. Our aim is to ensure that the Lord Jesus Christ is presented as the only hope to obtain forgiveness of sin, live a useful life and look forward to heaven with Him.

REACHING OUT
Christ's last command requires us to reach out to our world with His gospel. We seek to help fulfill that by publishing books that point people towards Jesus and help them develop a Christ-like maturity. We aim to equip all levels of readers for life, work, ministry and mission.

Books in our adult range are published in three imprints.

Christian Focus contains popular works including biographies, commentaries, basic doctrine and Christian living. Our children's books are also published in this imprint.

Mentor focuses on books written at a level suitable for Bible College and seminary students, pastors, and other serious readers. The imprint includes commentaries, doctrinal studies, examination of current issues and church history.

Christian Heritage contains classic writings from the past.

Christian Focus Publications, Ltd
Geanies House, Fearn,
Ross-shire, IV20 1TW, Scotland

info@christianfocus.com